GOODFELLOWS

THE CHAMPIONS OF ST. AMBROSE

RICK GOSSELIN

To Jim Johnson,

Once a Catholic League guy,
always a Catholic League guy —
even if you're on the other
side of the state.

Rick Gosselin

August Publications
Minneapolis, Minnesota

Regards -
Joe D'Angelo

GOODFELLOWS: THE CHAMPIONS OF ST. AMBROSE

August Publications
527 Marquette Av., Suite 800
Minneapolis, MN 55402
612.343.5207
augustpublications.com

ISBN 978-0-9752706-8-4

9 8 7 6 5 4 3 2 1

Designer (cover and interior): Natalie Nowytski
Cover photo by Kevin Reichard, football courtesy Tom Boisture

To Earl and Barbara Gosselin, St. Ambrose parents

TABLE OF CONTENTS

TABLE OF CONTENTS (CONT'D)

FOREWORD

I met Rick Gosselin for the first time in the press box of Arrowhead Stadium in 1989. I was in my first year as an assistant coach for the Kansas City Chiefs and Rick was covering the team for the Kansas City Star. What was unusual about that meeting was that it didn't take place on a game day, but on a day when there was no activity, not even a practice. I would later discover that Rick was a regular at the stadium, and that day we struck up a friendship that has lasted 20 years.

We hit it off almost immediately and ended up spending a lot of time talking in that press box in 1989. My first thought was that Rick was a little different than most writers that covered pro football. He wanted to know not only what had happened on the field, but why it happened. His columns didn't always focus on the obvious story line, more often touching on what made the star players great or who was doing a good job that the average person may not realize. I got the sense that it was more than a job for Rick. Sure, he wanted to inform the fans with his columns but he wanted to know some of these things because he was a fan.

I would come to find out that not only did he love football, but sports in general. That was perfect for me because I loved to talk sports, too. The more we talked over the ensuing months, the less we talked about the Chiefs and the more we talked about other players, other teams, other sports. It was great fun for me because I enjoy talking sports and, because we both grew up in Michigan, he knew a lot of players and coaches that I knew.

The next year Rick left Kansas City to write for the Dallas Morning News and, soon after that, I left to become the defensive coordinator for the Minnesota Vikings. But we would continue to talk regularly over the years. Sometimes we would talk about the Vikings defense but more often about what else was going on in the sports world. Because Rick went to Michigan State and I went to Minnesota we talked a lot about Big 10 sports. For both of us, though, our roots were in Michigan high school football. And that's where the special tie is for us in Goodfellows: The Champions of St. Ambrose. In this book, Rick tells the story of how St. Ambrose, a tiny Catholic high school on Detroit's East Side, came to grow into a football power in the state of Michigan.

St. Ambrose developed a rich football tradition in the late 1950s and remained dominant in the 1960s. However, by the time I graduated from high school in 1973, St. Ambrose was no longer a powerhouse able to compete with the larger schools. I was amazed to find out, though, that many of the coaches I had competed against in college and professional football had ties to that small high-school program. In fact, two of St. Ambrose's coaches, Tom Boisture and George Perles, would go on to help the New York Giants and Pittsburgh Steelers in six Super Bowl victories.

The book, though, is about more than just great coaches, championship trophies, and the little school that for years outplayed all the big boys. Rick looks at how they were able to do it, and then, what led to St. Ambrose's ultimate decline. He also paints a great picture of what it was like to grow up in Detroit at that time and what our society thought about high-school sports back then. It's also a very honest book—you'll see how rules were bent, and sometimes broken, to facilitate winning.

This book tells a great story of some tremendous athletes and great coaches. It chronicles some of the most dominant high-school football ever played in the state of Michigan. If you're a football historian, you'll recognize many of the names that are mentioned. But, more than anything, it tells of how hard work, team spirit and community support combined to create a special era at a very special place — St. Ambrose High School.

— *Tony Dungy*

Tony Dungy led the Indianapolis Colts to a Super Bowl victory on February 4, 2007, the first NFL championship for an African-American coach. A native of Jackson, Mich., he held assistant coaching positions with the University of Minnesota, Pittsburgh Steelers, Kansas City Chiefs and Minnesota Vikings and also served as the head coach of the Tampa Bay Buccaneers. Before becoming a coach, Dungy played three seasons in the NFL. He's the author of Uncommon: Finding Your Path to Significance.

INTRODUCTION

Among the many things that attracted me to the head coaching job of the Detroit Lions was the incredible loyalty and support of the Detroit sports fans. For as long as I can remember, Detroit had a reputation as one of the best sports cities in America — a place where sports truly matter to its people. Since my first day on the job with the Lions, I've experienced this passion first-hand. Not a day goes by when I don't come in contact with someone who is not only passionate about the Lions, but about all the teams in our community.

My hometown of Baltimore is very similar. Growing up in the 1960s and 1970s, sports were as much a part of the fabric of our community as faith and family. But it wasn't just the Colts, Orioles and Terps who were held in such high regard. It started at the high school level at places like Calvert Hall, Loyola, and my alma mater, Mt. St. Joseph High. Those schoolboy stars were bigger-than-life to youngsters like me.

I could never imagine sports being as important to its community as it was to ours in Baltimore. I was wrong. After reading Rick Gosselin's remarkable story, *Goodfellows: The Champions of St. Ambrose*, I not only have a better appreciation of why Detroit is such a passionate sports town, but I also now have a better understanding for the origin of that passion.

It started at the high-school level. At places like St. Ambrose. What the Cavaliers accomplished during those years on the football fields of Detroit will likely never be duplicated. David not only beat Goliath — David became Goliath.

Rick not only did an amazing job telling this story, but he did so in a way that causes you to feel like you are a part of the story. Close your eyes and you are there. You feel like you are a member of the St. Ambrose family. You are walking the halls of St. Ambrose. You are at Mass with the entire team — in full uniform, no less — just hours before a huge game. You are on the sideline cheering on your teammates against rivals Royal Oak Shrine, Redford St. Mary and Servite.

It's been said that "you can never go home again." That may be true for some, but after reading this book, I was home again. And I was a kid again — back in Baltimore watching that annual Thanksgiving Day game between Calvert Hall and Loyola.

My dad attended Calvert Hall and played for a football coach by the name of George Young — the same George Young who would go on to become the General Manager of the New York Giants and lead them to two Super Bowl titles. One of his most trusted personnel men for those Super Bowl teams was Tom Boisture. Yes, the same Tom Boisture who became head coach of the St. Ambrose Cavaliers in 1956 when this amazing journey — and story — began.

If you played high-school football, you will love this book. If you grew up in Detroit, you will love this book. If you grew up in the '50s and '60s, you will love this book. It will bring back wonderful memories of a different time and place in our society and culture.

The names in this book will astonish you. All of whom played a part in this historical era of high school football in Detroit — names even a kid from Baltimore would recognize. Names like Tom Boisture and George Perles. And Bill McCartney, Lloyd Carr, Dave Debusschere, Fred Arbanas, Ted Sizemore, the Paciorek brothers, the Seymour brothers, Al Fracassa, Gary Danielson, and Tom Beer.

While many of the St. Ambrose football players went on to college and some to pro football, you get the feeling after reading this book that nothing compared to their days as a Cavalier. Nothing was bigger than playing in the Soup Bowl or the Goodfellow Game.

This story took me on a special journey to a place where I believe it will also take you — back home — and there's no better place or feeling than that. Thanks Rick, for taking me home again.

— *Jim Schwartz*

Jim Schwartz was hired as the head coach of the Detroit Lions on January 15, 2009. A native of Baltimore, Md., he played football at Georgetown University and earned a degree in economics. He coached in college at North Carolina Central and Colgate before entering the NFL as a scout with the Cleveland Browns in 1993. He served as an assistant coach in the NFL with the Baltimore Ravens and Tennessee Titans before becoming head coach of the Lions.

ACKNOWLEDGMENTS

In the 1990s, as the NFL columnist for the *Dallas Morning News*, I would visit the training camps of the NFC East teams that competed against the Dallas Cowboys. That meant I'd spend a few nights each summer in Albany, N.Y., with the New York Giants. I always set aside an evening on those trips for dinner with the team's personnel director, Tom Boisture.

Boisture was the head football coach at St. Ambrose when I attended grade school there. His football teams took me through the fifth grade. We'd talk about the school, the parish, the priests and nuns over dinner, and he would regale me with tales of his football team. After several dinners and countless anecdotes, I concluded the story of the dramatic rise and fall of the St. Ambrose football team deserved to be written.

I spent the better part of six NFL offseasons in the 2000s researching this project. I found it an intriguing challenge trying to recreate conversations and events that took place 40 and 50 years ago. The memories of my subjects weren't as sharp in 2005 as they may have been in 1965.

But I figured the more participants I interviewed, the clearer the story would become. I hope I succeeded in this portrayal of the St. Ambrose football program during that 20-year period from 1952-71. The centerpiece of the story, of course, is the 1959 Goodfellow Game, which remains one of the great upsets in Michigan prep football history. All along I targeted publication of the book for 2009 — the 50th anniversary of that upset.

My thanks to Dolores Boisture, the wife of Tom Boisture; Carolyn Huber, the cousin of Dave Vitali; and the late Margaret Van Goethem, the mother of Mike, Bob and Gerry Van Goethem; for putting together meticulous scrapbooks back then that 40 and 50 years later would provide me a road map for this story.

My thanks to the newsmen from the *Detroit Free Press*, *News*, *Times* and *Michigan Catholic* who so passionately covered high school football during that era: Harvey Barcus, Joe Dowdall, Frank Guyott, Tom Jacobowski, Hal Schram and Ken Williams. Their stories in those scrapbooks freshened the memory and brought several of the games back to life for me.

My thanks to general manager Gerry Rauch and managing editor Marylyn Hewitt of the *Michigan Catholic* for graciously opening their archives to me. Also to Lynn Henning and Bill Haney, whose input and encouragement to a first-time author in the pursuit of a publisher was invaluable.

My thanks to Kevin Reichard and the folks at August Publications, who shared my passion for this project. Kevin, Erin Kangas and Natalie Nowytski embraced the book and were as committed to putting this story into print as I was. Also to Tony Dungy and Jim Schwartz for carving times out of their busy schedules to read the manuscript and offer their endorsements.

My thanks to the folks who run the Michigan high school web site, *http://michigan-football.com*, which I found to be invaluable for cross-checking scores and records. I also used the Wikipedia web site for some basic biographical details on Dave Bonior and Fr. Charles Coughlin. My thanks to Ron Pesch, the historian for the Michigan High School Athletic Association, for digging up the state rankings and all-state teams from that era.

My thanks to St. Ambrose head coaches Tom Boisture, Joe Carruthers, George Perles, Harvey Heitman and assistants Larry Bielat, Bill David and Jim Louwers for emptying their memory banks into my tape recorder.

My thanks to St. Ambrose Cavaliers Ron Albers, Lloyd Bayer, Tom Beer, Tom Bialk, Greg Bringard, Dave Brozo, Jack Cairo, Tony Carducci, Mickey Carter, Jim Conahan, Norm Cure, Joe D'Angelo, Guy Dinverno, Jim Dinverno, John Dziurman, Ray Federspiel, Bill Fournier, Pete Genord, Mike Goff, Tony Gramer, Greg Hacias, Paul Hayner, Marshall Houle, John Jambor, Larry Lantzy, Jim Laskowski, Bill Lenhard, Ray Malcoun, Gary Nowak, Skip Paoletti, Pete Piazza, Cory Richardson, Gerry Stogniew, Mike Taormino, Gerry Van Goethem, Mike Van Goethem, Mike Ward and Dave Vitali — without whom there would be no book to write.

My thanks to St. Ambrose foes Dave Brazil, Regis Cavender, Al Fracassa, Ross MacDonald and Roger Parmentier for their memories of that era. My thanks also to Jerry Burns, Chuck Fairbanks, Doug Graber, Joe Greene and Jerry Reese from my NFL rolodex.

My thanks to St. Ambrose pastor Fr. Timothy Pelc for providing an historical perspective on the parish, plus Tom Baulch, Doug Delaney, Jorjean Edmiston, Tim Griffin, Wayne Joseph, Rick Mahon, Mark Michael, Sr. Mary Ellen Plummer and Kathy Tobianski for their memories of growing up in the parish.

My thanks (again) to Beer, Boisture, Bringard, Brozo, Conahan, D'Angelo, Dziurman, Goff, Joseph, Malcoun, Gari Michaels and Vitali, who dug deep into their trunks and provided the photos and artifacts used throughout the pages of this book.

My thanks to my uncle Patrick Pearse Costello, whose passion for writing spilled over into my life. Also to Ellen Sullivan, who arrived at the right time in my life.

Lastly, but especially, my thanks to my family for a lifetime of support. My father Earl, who blessed me with his love of sports. My mother Barbara, who inspired me to chase my dreams. My older brother Tom, who taught me how to compete in sports and in life. My sisters Mary Anne, Kathy and Karen and brother Tim, with whom I shared the four-block walks and later the 22-block drives to St. Ambrose. And my youngest brother Sean, who established his own football identity at Bishop Gallagher as an honorable mention All-Catholic selection in 1982.

Rick Gosselin
St. Ambrose Class of 1969

GIANT KILLERS

There was a knock on the front door at 1358 Maryland that spring afternoon.

It was 1956 and Tom and Dolores Boisture and their infant daughter had been settling into their middle-class Grosse Pointe Park bungalow for almost a year. Dolores answered the knock and through the screen door saw a squatty man with thinning hair. He wanted to see Tom.

Dolores went to find her husband in the back of the house.

"A Mr. John Tobianski is at the door," Dolores told him.

"Who's he?" Tom asked.

"The maintenance man at St. Ambrose," Dolores answered.

So Tom retreated to the door to visit with a janitor — and one of the most unique football dynasties in Michigan high school history was born.

That brief chat in the living room of the Boisture home paved the way for Tom's hiring as the head football coach at St. Ambrose High School. He would coax the small Class C school on Detroit's lower East side to the Catholic League championship game in his very first season as coach in 1956. Boisture would launch St. Ambrose into the state rankings by 1958 — and the Cavaliers would become regulars.

St. Ambrose became known as Giant Killers in 1959, toppling Class A power Detroit Cooley in the annual Goodfellow Game that pitted the city's parochial and public school champions. It was the first time St. Ambrose had ever negotiated a football season without a defeat — but it wouldn't be the last.

Over a nine-year period from 1959 through 1967, the Cavaliers would post a 64-8-3 record, winning six conference titles, five Catholic League titles, five city titles with a perfect 5-0 record in Goodfellow Games, and four state championships. Little St. Ambrose would enjoy four 9-0 seasons during that stretch with two other seasons ending with a single loss.

Little St. Ambrose? Indeed. The school didn't have its own football field. It didn't have its own practice field. The locker room was carved out between two classrooms in the school's basement, and the coaching office was a converted coal bin. But football success pulsated from that three-story building with fewer than 400 high school students, more than half of whom were girls. From 1959-67, the St. Ambrose graduating classes ranged from 75-99 students. Again, half of them were girls.

But the boys...the boys were special. St. Ambrose would produce five football All-Americas and 12 all-state performers. Many would go on to play major-college football on the campuses of Houston, Michigan, Michigan State, Nebraska, Wyoming and, locally, at the University of Detroit. Two St. Ambrose products, ends Tom Beer and Gary Nowak, would extend their careers into the National Football League. Two of the coaches, Boisture and his successor George Perles, would go on to win a combined six Super Bowl rings in the NFL.

Boisture won his two championship rings in 1986 and 1990 as the director of personnel for the New York Giants. Perles won his four rings as first the defensive line coach, then defensive coordinator and finally the assistant head coach of the Pittsburgh Steelers, all in the 1970s. Perles would return to his alma mater Michigan State in the 1980s and coach the Spartans to seven bowl games, highlighted by a Rose Bowl victory over Southern Cal in 1988.

But the football glory enjoyed by Boisture and Perles outlived the prosperity at St. Ambrose. The descension of this prep dynasty came as rapidly as the ascension.

Joe Carruthers succeeded Perles as the head coach at St. Ambrose in 1965 and produced the last in the series of Catholic, city and state champions in 1966. The final hurrah came in 1967 when St. Ambrose finished in a three-way tie for the Catholic Double-A championship with Dearborn Divine Child and Detroit Servite. Divine Child, led by future NFL quarterback Gary Danielson, would go on to win its first Goodfellow Game and finish with a No. 4 state ranking among Class B schools with a 8-1 mark. The only blemish on its record was a 25-14 thrashing from Class C St. Ambrose.

But by 1970, St. Ambrose plummeted to Catholic League patsy with a 1-7 record. In 1971, the Cavaliers failed to score a single point in losing all eight of their games. They were outscored 158-0. In 1972, the school was shuttered by the Archdiocese of Detroit.

But what a run the little Giant Killers on Detroit's East side staged in the 1960s, regularly defeating teams that were three, four and five times larger by enrollment.

"When I think about a great high school program, I think about St. Ambrose," said Doug Graber, himself a product of the Detroit Catholic League who would spend 31 years of his life coaching in high school, college, the NFL and NFL Europe. "They only had 400 students — but 200 had to be football players and I bet most were recruited (by colleges). They were like the (Vince Lombardi) Packers (of the 1960s). When you heard, 'St. Ambrose,' you thought…. Wow.

"Years later when I went to coach at Michigan Tech I recruited Detroit. I visited St. Ambrose. I saw the school. You'd walk in and wonder, 'How the hell could they do all that here?'"

What they did and how they did it all started on the front porch of a home at 1358 Maryland.

IDENTITY

St. Ambrose suffered from an identity crisis.

It was a crossover Catholic parish with families residing in both Detroit and Grosse Pointe Park. Which essentially made St. Ambrose a crossover parish between the middle and upper class.

Grosse Pointe Park was the first of the five monied Grosse Pointe suburbs lining Lake St. Clair, which feeds into of the Detroit River. Grosse Pointe Park sat at the mouth of the river with Grosse Pointe City, Farms, Woods, and Shores strung along the Lake St. Clair shoreline. The closer the homes were to the water, the farther the homes were from the Detroit city line — and the more expensive the homes.

Old money ran deep in the Pointes. The Fords of Ford Motor Company fame lived there. So did the Dodges, another historic automobile family. Buffalo Bills owner and NFL Hall of Famer Ralph Wilson and local sporting legends Kirk Gibson and Steve Yzerman all have called one of the Grosse Pointes home.

The deepest pockets were clustered along Lake Shore Drive, the crown jewel of the Pointes.

Jefferson Avenue was a main artery connecting downtown Detroit to the Pointes. It rolled through middle-class Detroit neighborhood after middle-class Detroit neighborhood, past the Belle Isle bridge, past the Chrysler plant, past countless auto dealerships, gasoline stations, tire shops, party stores, bakeries, nickel-and-dimes, dry cleaners, bars, and diners.

When Jefferson Avenue arrived at the Detroit city line at Alter Road, lush green lawns suddenly started appearing. The property lots increased in size. Large front and back yards and long driveways became visible from Jefferson. Welcome to the Grosse Pointes. The money there was visible and evident. Pemberton, Lakepointe, Westchester, Balfour, Berkshire, Buckingham, Devonshire, Audubon, Whittier — even the Grosse Pointe street names carried a more regal tone than those intersecting Jefferson on the Detroit side: Ashland, Conner, Drexel, Eastlawn, Fairview, and Lycaste.

The deeper you traveled into the Pointes along Jefferson Avenue, the brighter the affluence would glow. At the first sign of water, Jefferson Avenue magically transformed itself into Lake Shore Drive. Around Fisher Road, as Jefferson began bending north, Lake Shore Drive started appearing on the mailboxes and street signs. To the right of Lake Shore Drive was the wet majesty of Lake St. Clair. To the left sat mansions on high offering spectacular waterfront views. On a summer day you could watch the sailboats bobbing on the lake. Farther out, you could see the freighters lugging their cargo in and out of the Great Lakes.

But when Lake Shore Drive reached the St. Clair Shores city limit, as the road headed back inland away from the water, it once again became Jefferson Avenue. It was a telling reminder to all those on the East Side the glamour of the lakefront belonged to the Grosse Pointes.

In all chronology documenting its football successes, the school was identified as Grosse Pointe St. Ambrose. And that's where the identity crisis surfaced.

The St. Ambrose school building housing all 12 grades straddled the city limits. It sat on a plot of land on Hampton Road between Wayburn and Alter. Half the school was in Detroit, the other half in Grosse Pointe Park. The convent housing the nuns teaching at the school was on Alter Road in Detroit. St. Ambrose

Church and the rectory housing the priests of the parish were on Hampton in Grosse Pointe Park. The hall, where the school staged its homecoming dances, pep rallies, bake sales, school carnivals, grade-school basketball games, and clandestine football practices, was located on Maryland in Grosse Pointe Park, kitty-corner from the rectory. In 1965, when St. Ambrose erected a second building to house its grade school, it sat on Alter Road across the street from the convent.

So St. Ambrose was as much Detroit as it was Grosse Pointe. But well before its football team ever advanced to a Goodfellow Game, St. Ambrose parish opted to embrace its blue-collar Detroit roots, not the affluence of the Grosse Pointes.

The Archdiocese of Detroit named Father Francis Van Antwerp the pastor of St. Ambrose in 1937. He had a friend in a very high place — the Detroit City Council. His brother Eugene served Detroit there for 31 years from 1932 until his death in 1962. He spent 29 years on the city council and two more in the mayoral chair.

Naturally, when Fr. Van Antwerp was looking out for the best interests of his parish, he looked Westward toward Detroit — not eastward toward the Pointes.

"There were a lot of city services and ties that came his way because of his connections with the city of Detroit," said Fr. Timothy Pelc, who became the pastor of St. Ambrose in 1986 and served in that capacity into the next century. "At that time it was Detroit that was well-organized, well-funded and offered so many more city services. Grosse Pointe wasn't anything by comparison.

"The name of the game back then was how much Detroit property could you amass because it was a better-run city. It had more money, more clout. But that all changed after the [1967] riots. As soon as the neighborhood improves, it becomes [the neighboring] St. Clare Parish. When St. Clare was established, Father VanAntwerp didn't argue. He was fine with that. The thinking was Detroit was the place to be, not the suburbs."

Photo courtesy Dave Vitali

Father Francis Van Antwerp

So the St. Ambrose parish extended only seven blocks into the Grosse Pointes to Balfour. On Wayburn, Maryland, Lakepointe, and Beaconsfield north of Jefferson, homes sat side-by-side in a cabbage-patch clump. So close were the homes you could hear what was playing on the television next door. On Beaconsfield and Nottingham south of Jefferson, two- and four-family flats were the residence of choice.

If a blue-collar existence could be found in any of the Grosse Pointes, it was that five- or six-block stretch east of Alter Road providing the welcome mat of the St. Ambrose parish.

There was wealth in the parish. Again, the closer to the water, the more expensive the home. Windmill Pointe Drive along the eastern edge of Grosse Pointe Park offered a handful of mansions offering magnificent waterfront views of Lake St. Clair. Homes approaching Windmill Pointe Drive at the foot of Pemberton, Lakepointe, and Middlesex also stood as testimonials to an upper-class existence in Grosse Pointe Park.

The perception of Grosse Pointe was white collar. Money. Prosperity. The *Grosse Pointe* attached in every public reference to St. Ambrose smacked of elitism. But make no mistake about it — the parish, the school and the football team were built on the blue-collar grit of Detroit.

"The cosmopolitan nature of St. Ambrose was a conscious embracing of Detroit," Fr. Pelc said.

But Fr. Van Antwerp wanted to embrace something beyond the parish's Detroit roots. He developed a strong rooting interest in the Detroit Lions, Tigers, and Red Wings. From 1935-50, Detroit celebrated a combined seven championships by its three hometown teams.

Fr. Van Antwerp appreciated the prestige a championship team could bring to a fan base. The east-side high-school sporting scene was being dominated in the 1950s by basketball schools at Detroit Austin and Grosse Pointe St. Paul. Fr. Van Antwerp saw an opening for a football power — and he wanted St. Ambrose to seize it.

But Fr. Van Antwerp didn't know how. Enter Father George Rozman.

03

REDFORD ST. MARY

St. Mary of Redford was all St. Ambrose aspired to be. St. Mary was all any parish high school in the city of Detroit in the 1950s aspired to be, for that matter.

St. Mary was one of the oldest parishes in the Archdiocese of Detroit, founded in 1843 on a strip of land along Grand River Avenue in Redford, bordering the northwest tip of Detroit. The school was built in 1920 and, over time, surrounding farmland was sold off to the city of Detroit, which absorbed the parish.

By the 1940s, the school was identified less by its location than for its excellence on the gridiron. The St. Mary Rustics had become a parochial juggernaut. In a 12-year span from 1947-1958, Redford St. Mary won eight Catholic League titles and appeared in eight Goodfellow Games. The Rustics won four city championships, whipping Western in 1951, University of Detroit High in 1952 and 1954 and Southeastern in 1957.

Tom Boisture was aware of St. Mary's prowess long before he moved into the St. Ambrose parish, long before he became a high-school coach on the city's East side. Tom's older brother Dan served as the head coach of St. Mary in the 1950s.

Tom Boisture himself attended a West-side Catholic high school, Holy Redeemer, and went on to play college ball at Mississippi State. He played his first two seasons under Murray Warmath and his final year under Darrell Royal in 1954.

But his senior season was interrupted. That October Boisture received a call from his brother. Their mother Mabel had been diagnosed with terminal cancer.

"You'd better come home," Dan said.

During his afternoons in Detroit, Tom would troop over to St. Mary to help his brother coach the Rustics, who were preparing for the Catholic League championship game — the Soup Bowl — against Detroit St. Anthony.

A major-college lineman himself at Mississippi State, Boisture donned the pads for one practice with the Rustics. That was a mistake. He lined up across from a sophomore end by the name of Fred Arbanas, who would go on to become an All-Big Ten performer at Michigan State and the tight end on the all-time, All-AFL team with the Kansas City Chiefs.

"He almost killed me," Boisture recalled. "I couldn't believe a 10th grader could hit that hard."

Boisture remained in Detroit for three weeks as his mother's condition stabilized. She would live for another five years. So Tom returned to Mississippi State for the final weeks of his own football season.

"I knew I wasn't going to play much because of all the (practice) time I missed," Boisture said. "But I knew had to get back to school. My brother suggested I transfer to University of Detroit."

But with a four-year investment in Mississippi State, Tom returned to Starkville to finish out his college football career and education. Dan finished out his own season at St. Mary as the city runner-up, losing the Goodfellow Game to University of Detroit High, 23-20.

Dan Boisture would post a 37-5-2 record in his five seasons at St. Mary, suffering only two losses to Catholic schools. Fr. Van Antwerp admired what St. Mary had built from afar. So did every other parish pastor in the Archdiocese.

Fr. Rozman was able to admire from up close. In his capacity as athletic director at St. Mary in the 1940s, he laid the groundwork for that dynasty on the city's west side.

But in 1952, three Goodfellow Games into his tenure at St. Mary, the Archdiocese of Detroit transferred Fr. Rozman to the East side of town. The Van Antwerp dream of a football power for his parish took a giant step toward reality with the arrival of Fr. Rozman at St. Ambrose.

04

GROUNDWORK

Fr. George Rozman was not a patient man.

Fueled by his successes at St. Mary, Fr. Rozman was in a rush to win at St. Ambrose. He churned through three coaches in his first four seasons on the east side: George Verdonckt, John Thursby, and Joe Flood. The strength of the Catholic League remained on the city's west side, where St. Mary was rumbling along to Goodfellow Games in 1952, 1954 and 1955.

Rozman realized a quick turnaround was not imminent. But only a man of deep faith could believe such a turnaround was even possible, much less imminent. St. Ambrose was not St. Mary. For starters, St. Ambrose was a Second Division Catholic League program. The Cavaliers weren't even competing on the same shelf as St. Mary.

St. Ambrose did not have its own football field. The school rented out Mack Park for its home games. A converted baseball field, Mack Park hosted Detroit's Negro Leagues entry, the Stars, in the 1920s. It was located only four miles west of St. Ambrose down Mack Avenue — but culturally it was light years away from the Grosse Pointes. Mack Park was on Fairview Avenue in a racially diverse neighborhood. This was 1952. St. Ambrose would not hire its first African-American teacher nor enroll its first African-American student until 1966.

The Cavaliers didn't have a practice field, either. St. Ambrose rented space on the playground at Defer, a public elementary school six blocks away in Grosse Pointe Park. Defer was large enough for four compact baseball diamonds, which housed the Grosse Pointe Park Little League every spring. It was not unusual in the fall to see three separate St. Ambrose football teams practicing at Defer, representing the high school, junior varsity, and grade school.

If you were walking from St. Ambrose to Defer, you'd head north up Wayburn a block, then east on St. Paul four blocks, then north up Nottingham one final block. And that's how the players would get to practice when Fr. Rozman arrived — by foot. St. Ambrose didn't own a school bus back in 1952. Clickity-clack was the sound of football cleats on pavement for that hike to practice. Some upperclassmen drove their cars.

There also wasn't a football locker room at St. Ambrose. The players would shower in the boys' bathroom in the basement of the school after practice. The equipment was stored in a room adjacent to the shower.

Fr. Rozman knew he would one day need, at minimum, a bus and lockerroom to become competitive in football with other parish schools like St. Mary, St. Catherine, St. Anthony, and Shrine — much less the all-boys schools like Catholic Central, DeLaSalle, and the University of Detroit.

But to compete, St. Ambrose would need money. The Dad's Club had been around since 1950, founded by parishioners Joseph Griffin, Thomas Krass, and William Ruthenberg. That organized the parish's effort to financially support its football team. But the group needed direction.

Fr. Rozman was tired of watching the school field a second-class product. If you want to be first class, you must act first class. So at his initial meeting with the Dad's Club, Fr. Rozman carted all the football equipment into the school's hall for the men of the parish to see — helmets, shoulder pads, cleats, pants, jerseys.

"I'm burning it," announced Fr. Rozman as he piled it all onto the floor. "We're getting all new equipment. Now go out and raise the money for it."

Father George Rozman

Photo courtesy Dave Vitali

From that point on, money would gush for football. The more the school won, the more freely the cash would flow. The Dad's Club had deep pockets. So did the parish. Fr. Van Antwerp became the team's guardian angel when money ran a wee bit short.

"I would imagine some of it came out of the [Sunday] collection baskets," Tom Boisture mused.

Money would solve any problems off the field. But on the field, Fr. Rozman continued to tinker with other problems. He inherited Verdonckt, whose family owned a local bakery. Rozman replaced him in 1953 with John Thursby, who was a teacher at Grosse Pointe High. Thursby played college ball at Purdue and was well-liked by the players.

"John was a brute of a man," said John Jambor, who quarterbacked St. Ambrose in the mid-1950s. "He was very much a players' coach because he had been a player himself. But he instilled a lot of discipline in the program."

Thursby coached the Cavaliers to a 6-1-2 record in 1953 at the Second Division level, then a 7-1 mark despite a step up in competition in the First Division in 1954. But Thursby was being pressured from both sides demanding a full-time commitment. Grosse Pointe High wanted him to focus on teaching; St. Ambrose wanted him focusing on coaching.

The money, then as now, was in the public schools, so Thursby opted to teach. He left St. Ambrose after two seasons, and Fr. Rozman replaced him with Joe Flood in 1955. Thursby wouldn't be the last coach St. Ambrose would lose to the Grosse Pointes.

The Cavaliers floundered under Flood, finishing 2-4. He didn't endear himself to the players as Thursby had.

"He was a knowledgeable football guy but I didn't think much of his training techniques," said Mike Taormino, who also played under Thursby and Boisture. "If we played on Sunday afternoon, we'd go out on Saturday morning in pads and hit at full speed. We had a couple key injuries in those Saturday practices, which was kind of ridiculous. It was all blood and guts on Saturday mornings. It was tough. If you didn't go full speed, you were doing laps. He was a tough customer."

There were no Catholic League championships during the first four seasons of the Fr. Rozman era, but there were strides taken in that direction.

Thursby ambitiously recruited players from other grade schools, expanding the student base beyond the parish kids. He scouted grade schools playing Catholic Youth Organization (CYO) football and laid the pipeline that would turn St. Juliana and St. Veronica into bountiful suppliers to the St. Ambrose talent pool.

It was Thursby's recruits who would provide the nucleus of the St. Ambrose team that reached its first Soup Bowl in 1956.

Thursby also drove home the point to his players that football was more than an after-school activity.

"He emphasized multi-sports," said Gerry Stogniew, who grew up in the St. Ambrose parish and would start in high school for Thursby, Flood, and Boisture. "He got us looking at football as being more than three months out of the year. He got us involved in other sports with the idea that it would make us better football players.

"As a freshman, even though I knew nothing about baseball, basketball, and track, I had to play to stay in shape for football."

By 1956, the money was in place. So was the recruiting. There was a commitment from both the players and the school administration to succeed. But one last element needed to be locked into place.

AUSTIN

Tom Boisture was right.

After his nearly month-long absence from campus in the fall of 1954, Boisture wasn't going to see any playing time upon his return to Mississippi State for the remainder of his own football season. He practiced during the week with the Bulldogs but did not play on Saturdays in the final two games of the season against traditional rivals LSU and Ole Miss.

But Darrell Royal gave Boisture and a handful of graduating seniors a taste of coaching, inviting them to assist during Mississippi State's spring practice in 1955. Boisture worked with the offensive and defensive linemen and thoroughly enjoyed the experience. He graduated that spring with a degree in education and realized what he liked teaching most was football. So pursuing a coaching career would forge a marriage of his two passions, football and teaching.

With the encouragement of Royal, Boisture applied for a string of junior-college coaching positions in Mississippi that spring but didn't land any of them. Then came another telephone call from his brother Dan in Detroit.

"Austin is looking for a coach," Dan said. "They're a brand new high school. This [1955] is going to be their first senior class. Are you interested?"

Tom was definitely interested. He needed a job. He became a husband and father before graduating from college, so he had a family to support. Dan drove across town to visit with the Augustinian fathers about their coaching vacancy.

Having one of the Catholic League's most prominent coaches standing in your rectory carried considerable clout with the Austin decision-makers. Dan Boisture told the priests how Tom had worked with his Catholic League champion Rustics that fall and he believed his younger brother had a bright future in coaching.

"Bring him in," the priests told Dan.

Tom flew back to Detroit the next week for his interview and brought more to the Austin campus than just a strong family recommendation. He brought letters of recommendation from three major-college coaches — Murray Warmath at the University of Minnesota, Darrell Royal at Mississippi State and Duffy Daugherty at Michigan State.

Boisture had played for both Warmath and Royal at Mississippi State, and Daugherty had been on the Redford St. Mary campus to recruit Dan Boisture's star players. He would one day sign Fred Arbanas to attend Michigan State and also had his eye on Dan down the road as a possible assistant coach. Sure, Duffy would write a letter of recommendation for Dan's younger brother Tom, no problem at all.

For someone with so little coaching experience, Tom Boisture had compiled an impressive list of advocates. He was hired as the head football and baseball coach at Austin.

"I went right from college into high-school coaching," Boisture said. "At the time that was highly unusual."

It may have been the right opportunity, but Boisture came to realize it was definitely the wrong situation. He would coach the wrong two sports at the fledgling all-boys school. Austin coveted an identity as a basketball school.

Boisture finished 3-3 in his debut as a high-school football coach. He also reached the Catholic League championship game in baseball at Briggs Stadium, the home of the Detroit Tigers, riding the right arm of a strapping underclassman by the name of Dave DeBusschere. It wouldn't be Boisture's last coaching visit to Briggs Stadium, which would later be known as Tiger Stadium.

That same Dave DeBusschere would lead Austin to a state basketball championship as a senior and go on to become one of a small handful of professional two-sport athletes in American sports history. He pitched in the big leagues for the Chicago White Sox in the 1960s and was inducted into the Naismith Basketball Hall of Fame in 1983 following a 12-year NBA career with the Detroit Pistons and New York Knickerbockers, playing on two championships teams.

But basketball greatness wasn't going to help Boisture win any football games. After the basketball season he talked Austin point guard Don Messey into coming out for football.

"He could jump to the moon," Boisture recalled. "He was an outstanding athlete who would have been my quarterback. He could throw it a mile and he could run. We ran the option and we'd have killed people. I thought he'd give us a chance to win the [Catholic] Central Division championship. That's how good he was."

But Boisture had him for only a handful of workouts that spring. His football career ended before it could start. The Austin basketball coaches advised him to focus his time and energy on hoops, not football. Boisture knew then he'd be doomed to mediocrity for however long he coached at Austin.

"This is a basketball school," Boisture told himself. "I can see that now. I'll get the leftovers. I won't get the athlete who's a good basketball player that may want to play for the football team."

But a job is a job, so Boisture resolved to spend another year or two or three at Austin — however long it would take to prove himself as a coach and improve his marketability.

The Boisture family had moved into an affordable section of Grosse Pointe Park near the Detroit city limits in the summer of 1955. It was about a five-mile drive to Austin but just a three-block walk to St. Ambrose, where the Boistures attended church every Sunday. But football season had passed and Boisture had not yet registered in the parish. He intended to do so at the conclusion of Austin's baseball season.

So one June day Boisture strolled down Maryland to the St. Ambrose rectory, which doubled as the parish office. He rapped on the door and who should answer but Fr. George Rozman. Both men saw a familiar face.

"Aren't you the priest who was the athletic director at St. Mary's of Redford when I was in high school back in '49?" Boisture asked the priest.

"Sure am," responded Fr. Rozman, who then welcomed Boisture into his office for a visit.

"Weren't you at Austin this past year?" Fr. Rozman asked Boisture.

"I'm still there," Boisture said.

The two spent almost three hours talking about football, St. Mary of Redford, and Boisture's brother Dan. Finally Boisture registered for the parish and walked home.

A few hours later, the janitor was standing on his front porch.

JANITOR

To say John Tobianski was merely the head of maintenance at St. Ambrose would be understating his value to the parish — and to the football team. Tobianski was as much a fixture on Hampton Road in the 1950s and 1960s as the buildings for the church, rectory, and school.

Tobianski, his wife and five kids lived at 1016 Maryland in the home next door to the parish hall. In fact, the Tobianski home had once been a part of the St. Ambrose parochial campus. It was the original rectory, housing the parish priests until 1947 when they moved across the street into the building on Hampton.

The Tobianski family moved from Hamtramck in 1950, and the children all had their own rooms in the new house. There were more rooms than family members. It was a mansion hidden inside a home, with seven bedrooms and four bathrooms. There were two garages out back, plus enough gravel space in the yard to park two school busses.

There was also a system of tunnels underneath the street connecting the Tobianski home to the hall, church, rectory, and school. The tunnels would come in handy later when the football team was emerging as a powerhouse. The tunnels gave Tobianski easy access to any of the parish buildings, which allowed him to address any problem at any hour. And there were problems.

"Any time they needed something or somebody, they'd call my dad at any time of the night," said Kathy Tobianski, the second youngest of the children who would later become a cheerleader for the football team. "I remember once getting a phone call around dinner time. One of the nuns got her finger caught in the mixer, and he was the first person they thought of to get over there and help this nun. They would call for anything — if there was no heat or some other malfunction."

John Tobianski would lock up the church at night. He'd lock up the school. In the winter he'd stoke the boilers providing heat to all of the buildings. He maintained the parish grounds. He drove the school bus. He washed Fr. Van Antwerp's car. He served as a trainer for the football team. Anything needing to be done at the parish, John Tobianski did. That's how he earned his paycheck from St. Ambrose.

But Tobianski earned his respect with his ears. He listened. He became a confidante of the priests, nuns, coaches, and players. He was a man of few words.

"I was a little chatterbox in the second grade," Kathy Tobianski said. "The nun I had then was a little fed up with me. So one day I was chatting away and she went and got my dad. He walked in and stood at my desk. My back was to him because I was fooling around.

"All of a sudden I turned and there he was. Everyone got quiet and I was mortified. Then he walked back out again. He never said a word. Just looked at me and left. My dad tended to be quiet. He didn't say a whole lot. He didn't share his feelings much but, boy, you could sure see them on his face."

When asked, Tobianski did offer his opinions. Fr. Van Antwerp asked often. So did the football coaches. He became a trusted voice, adviser and friend. George Perles would name his middle son John after Tobianski. Joe Carruthers chose Tobianski to be the godfather for his son Kirk, who would become an All-America linebacker at Florida State.

When Tobianski did speak, the good of the parish was always at heart. He became the conscience of St. Ambrose.

John Tobianski

Photo courtesy Tom Boisture

"John was a saint," Tom Beer said. "He was Mr. St. Ambrose."

Fr. George Rozman sat down with Tobianski that spring afternoon in 1956 after visiting with Boisture in the rectory. In his capacity as Mr. St. Ambrose, Tobianski took it upon himself to hike down Maryland, climb the steps onto the Boisture porch and knock on the door.

Tobianski introduced himself to Boisture and asked if he had any interest in coming to St. Ambrose to coach the football team. Boisture told him he already had a job.

"We've lost Joe Flood," Tobianski said. "He's going into business."

During the three hours Boisture had visited with Fr. Rozman, it never came up in conversation that St. Ambrose was in need of a football coach. Tobianski had transformed himself from janitor to salesman.

"We've got everybody coming back," Tobianski said. "I can show you the [game] film."

Boisture said that wouldn't be necessary.

"I'm doing this on my own," Tobianski said. "I'm not doing this on behalf of the parish. But we'll give you $6,500."

That shocked Boisture.

"For what?" he asked.

"For coaching and teaching a couple of classes," Tobianski said.

Boisture was making $3,500 as the head coach at Austin.

"Now I'll have to think about that," Boisture conceded.

Then Tobianski started talking about the 1956 St. Ambrose football team.

"I'm not worried about players," Boisture said. "If you've got Fr. Rozman, you've got halfway decent players because I know his background."

Boisture asked if he would be allowed to bring in his own coaches. Tobianski told him Fr. Rozman would be open to that.

"Let me think about it," Boisture said.

"I'll come back tonight," Tobianski told him.

"That's fine," Boisture said. "I want to visit with my wife about this. But I'm definitely interested."

A few hours later, during a second visit from Tobianski, Boisture agreed to become the school's fourth football coach in five seasons.

"I'd like to come over and take a look at the facilities," Boisture said.

Tobianski tried to downplay them.

"I can show you the locker room and equipment room," Tobianski said, "but I'm just in the process of building your office. You have to understand it's a coal bin right now."

"Coal bin?" Boisture said.

"But we've got nothing but the best equipment," Tobianski said. "Football is tops. But we'd like to build a basketball team, too."

"So would I," Boisture said, "because I'll be coaching football, basketball, and baseball."

Tobianski asked Boisture if he wanted to go over any financial details.

"No, let's wait until I sign," Boisture said. "I trust you. I know Fr. Rozman's background and I trust him."

The next day Boisture drove to Austin. He could hear the lawn mowers so he walked out back where the school's principal and athletic director were cutting the grass of the practice field. Their football coach told them he was leaving.

"They couldn't believe it," Boisture said.

The two Augustinian priests asked why.

"You have a basketball school here," Boisture said.

Boisture returned home and made his second visit to the St. Ambrose rectory in two days, this time sitting down with Fr. Rozman to formally accept his new position.

"Whatever you want, you've got," Fr. Rozman said. "We've got good players and we should have a good team."

"Fine," Boisture said. "I know what you expect. I'm going to run the Split-T [offense], the same as I ran at Austin. If your quarterback is as good as Tobianski says he is, he'll be ideal for this offense."

The quarterback was as good as Tobianski said he was. And Austin hired Joe Flood to replace Boisture.

JAMBOR

If Tom Boisture was going to make St. Ambrose competitive with Redford St. Mary for Catholic League titles, he knew he would first have to make the Cavaliers competitive with St. Anthony for East side titles. Anything East of Woodward Avenue was considered the city's East side, west of Woodward the West side.

In the era of the Goodfellow Game from 1938-1955, only one parish school from the East side ever played for the city championship — St. Anthony. The Teutons twice reached the Goodfellow Game, losing in 1946 to Cooley but beating U. of D. High in 1949.

From 1952-55, St. Anthony played in three Catholic League championship games, known as the Soup Bowl, but each time lost to Redford St. Mary. The Soup Bowl was so named because it was sponsored by the Capuchin Soup Kitchen, a Catholic mission providing food and clothing to the needy.

One of the greatest athletes in Detroit prep history played for St. Anthony in that 27-20 Soup Bowl loss in 1952 — Dan Currie, who became an all-city performer in both basketball and football. He would go on to become an All-America linebacker at Michigan State and a Pro Bowl linebacker for the Green Bay Packers.

St. Anthony was the school with the players, tradition, and aura on the east side. So Boisture circled Oct. 12 on his first schedule as head coach at St. Ambrose — the night the Cavaliers would square off against the Teutons at Mack Park.

Because of his late arrival at St. Ambrose, Boisture did not have the chance to recruit any players. He coached under the same

Photo courtesy Dave Brozo/Gari Michaels

John Jambor

hardship at Austin in 1955. The challenge at both places was to win with someone else's team.

But Flood left Boisture a talented cast. And John Tobianski was correct in his assessment of the quarterback — John Jambor was mighty slick taking the snaps for St. Ambrose.

Barely a season into his high-school career, Boisture had not developed a personality as a coach yet. He did not have a preferred offensive and defensive system in place. So he fit the schemes to his players on the field. With Jambor as his star, the Cavaliers would throw the football in 1956.

Jambor had a rifle for an arm. If DeBusschere wasn't the best high-school pitcher in the city of Detroit, Jambor was. He would sign a contract out of high school with the Baltimore Orioles and pitch in their farm system. In his senior year he hurled St. Ambrose to a victory over mighty Hamtramck St. Ladislaus, which won four Catholic League baseball titles from 1954-58.

Jambor's arm would carry the hopes of St. Ambrose into the 1956 football season.

"We were a passing team," Jambor said. "Everyone was a grinding team back then except us. We had a lot of fast backs and receivers. We threw the ball around and had a lot of fun."

Boisture was anxious to see just how talented his team was, so he scheduled two preseason scrimmages against Catholic League powerhouses St. Mary of Redford and DeLaSalle. Boisture was anxious to square off against his brother Dan, and Fr. Rozman was anxious to revisit the West side. But the Cavaliers were no match for St. Mary's Rustics.

"That was a tough day," said Mike Taormino, who played in the St. Ambrose defensive front seven. "Boisture was leaning on us because he wanted to make a good showing. I'm sure he had been bragging about us to his brother."

The Cavaliers fared better against DeLaSalle, an all-boys school.

"We threw the ball pretty well that day," Jambor said. "I thought we kicked the shit out of them."

Fueled by its performance against DeLaSalle, St. Ambrose stormed off to a 3-0 start. Oct. 12 arrived and the Cavaliers proved they could compete with St. Anthony. But competing with the Teutons and beating the Teutons were two different tasks. St. Ambrose lost, 26-22. That left the two teams tied for first place in the Catholic Division East at the season's midway point with 3-1 records.

But St. Ambrose won out, ripping through St. Ladislaus, St. Florian, and St. Charles by a combined 106-13 score, to finish 6-1. St. Anthony was upset by St. Florian a week after the St. Ambrose game, forcing the Teutons to settle for a 5-2 record.

That gave the Cavaliers their first East-side title and a berth in the Soup Bowl against DeLaSalle, playing for their first Catholic League championship. Jambor was one of the city's best passers. He threw for 10 touchdowns in seven games that season. That doesn't seem like much until you consider Tobin Rote led the NFL that year with 18 TD passes in 12 games and NCAA passing champion John Brodie threw only 12 touchdowns in 10 games.

Jambor would have the added benefit of having already played DeLaSalle that fall. So there was an air of confidence at St. Ambrose. But it didn't last long.

On the Monday before the game, Tobianski showed up at the practice field with a couple of dead chickens.

"The players from DeLaSalle sent these over," Tobianski said.

"Everyone knew that was a bunch of bullshit," Jambor said.

The week would get worse.

"We put in six new plays for the game, all running plays," Jambor said. "But what can you do in 3-4 days? The team was flat all week. The practices were flat. Tom was flat. Everyone was uptight. Fr. Rozman was wound up like a violin string. He was so excited he had trouble serving Mass that week.

"The night before the game I'm at home and I'm wound up mentally. I remember telling my dad, 'We're flat as a pancake. Nothing's happening for us. We just aren't ready.' Maybe it was because it was the first time. None of us had ever been in the position to play for a city title before. We were the highest scoring team in the league and there seemed to be a lot of pressure on us."

The façade started to crack. A few of the Cavaliers missed curfew on the eve of the game. One final bad omen awaited them just before the start of the Soup Bowl. The Cavaliers were in the locker room receiving their final instructions from Boisture when someone pounded on the door and told them it was time to come out.

So the Cavaliers charged down the hill onto the field — except that the band was still playing the national anthem.

"It was awkward," Jambor said. "The band didn't know whether to stop playing the anthem or what. It was total confusion."

What followed was more confusion. Jambor threw three interceptions, and all were returned for touchdowns. The Cavaliers also lost three fumbles, suffered two blocked punts and went down in flames, 44-6. The DeLaSalle that St. Ambrose scrimmaged in August was not the same DeLaSalle that showed up to play the Soup Bowl in November.

"They killed our passing game," Jambor said. "They were blitzing before anyone knew what blitzing was. They brought everybody. They were crashing their ends and bringing a linebacker. Our blocking assignments got all screwed up. I was under pressure all night and just throwing the ball around the park."

Boisture emptied his bench in the second half. Fr. Rozman had ranted at the team during halftime and resumed his rant on the school bus after the game. He was convinced he had not seen his team's best effort, that some of the Cavaliers preferred partying to playing football.

"He was hot," Taormino said. "He fired the football at somebody on the bus. That's the only time I ever saw him get animated — and he had good reason. He was invested in that thing. He wanted to see us do well for his sake, for our sake and for the school's sake. We let him down. We let a lot of people down. It's a damn shame. We were a better team than that — but we got our ass kicked."

Halfway home, Fr. Rozman told Tobianski to pull the bus over at a party store.

"I want to buy them a case of beer," he said sarcastically.

It would be the last season Boisture would put his fate in the hands of players he did not recruit.

RECRUITING

Catholic parishes carved up the city of Detroit in the 1950s like a huge jigsaw puzzle. You couldn't travel 20 blocks in any direction without finding a Catholic church or school.

The St. Ambrose parish was bordered by St. Martin to the west, St. Clare to the east, and St. Juliana to the North. Those parishes were squeezed themselves by Assumption Grotto, St. Brendan, Guardian Angels, St. Jude, St. Matthew, Our Lady Queen of Peace, St. Paul, St. Philip, and St. Philomena. The next layer of parishes included St. Basil, Our Lady Star of the Sea, St. Joan of Arc, St. Jude, and St. Veronica.

Every parish had its own church, its own school and, more importantly to Tom Boisture, its own grade-school football team. Find a vacant field or a set of goalposts anywhere in the city of Detroit during the fall in the 1950s and it's likely you'd find a Catholic grade-school team either practicing football or playing a game. The Catholic Youth Organization (CYO), which operated out of the Archdiocese of Detroit offices, coordinated the massive program.

"That was a huge edge for the Catholic schools," said Roger Parmentier, a member of the Michigan High School Football Coaches Association Hall of Fame for building Detroit Public School League powerhouses at Cooley and Denby. "They got their kids playing organized football at the ages of 12-13. That's why their programs were so good. I didn't get them until they enrolled in high school.

"And the Catholic schools could bring in kids from any area of the city or state because they were paying [scholarships]. I was confined — all the public schools were confined — to the kids who lived in your district. I used to tell the kids, 'I can give you free tuition, free books, free everything — just come to the public schools.

"All those Catholic schools had the opportunity to build a powerhouse. But only someone who grew up Catholic would know that."

Boisture realized that early on. Because St. Ambrose was one of a handful of parishes on the near east side with both a grade school and high school, the Cavaliers started with a solid talent base. Toby David, a parishioner known as "Captain Jolly" on local Detroit television, coached the grade-school team for a stretch in the 1950s. So did Joseph Griffin, one of the founding fathers of the Dad's Club.

Larry Bringard was a St. Ambrose lifer, spending 12 years attending classes in that same school building on Hampton. He lived two blocks away from St. Ambrose on Ashland, south of Jefferson in the first house over the bridge. Bringard played grade-school football at St. Ambrose, so Joe Flood didn't even need to recruit him in 1955.

"It was a foregone conclusion if you played grade-school football at Ambrose you'd play high-school football there," said Pete Piazza, another of the unrecruited parish kids who would start for both the grade school in the 1950s and high school in the 1960s.

Bringard was the best player ever to come out of the parish. He became the school's first All-America player in 1958. His younger brother Greg, who walked those same two blocks to school for 12 years, became St. Ambrose's fourth All-America player in 1964.

Boisture knew he could be competitive on high-school fields with the talent from St. Ambrose grade school. But the parish kids alone couldn't take him where he wanted to go.

Photo courtesy Greg Bringard

Larry Bringard

"I didn't have enough at the grade school to carry me," Boisture said. "I knew I had to bring in another 16-17 kids."

Boisture knew he would need to recruit the best players from other grade schools to compete for Catholic League titles. But there were only so many hours in a day, and Boisture had a staff of only two assistant coaches. Even with Fr. Rozman and John Tobianski, a pair of formidable recruiters themselves, Boisture realized the magnitude of the challenge.

But Boisture figured out a way to be everywhere and evaluate all the best athletes in the CYO system — and it wouldn't take him away from any of his responsibilities as the head football coach at St. Ambrose. He signed up to become a basketball referee for CYO games.

"That gave me a chance to see all the kids and talk to them," Boisture said.

Boisture could identify the athleticism on the court. The star basketball players at the grade-school level were generally the star football players as well. He could identify the kids who operated best under pressure. He wanted to collect as many of them as possible. He also could identify the kids who were pains in the ass. He wanted to steer clear of them.

So Boisture would compile his list of coveted eighth graders and give it to Tobianski to set up recruiting nights.

"John wasn't shy at all," Boisture said. "He'd call their homes and was really good with the parents."

There'd be a couple of different recruiting nights each winter. For obvious reasons. Little St. Ambrose could offer something the East side all-boys Catholic schools Austin and Notre Dame and public schools Grosse Pointe and Denby could not — opportunity.

There's a chance a freshman football player would see the field at St. Ambrose, where there were only 200 boys in the entire school. A Grosse Pointe and Denby might have 200 boys in the freshman class.

"We never brought them all in at the same time," Boisture said. "We didn't want them to know who they'd be competing against. So we only brought in about a dozen at a time. Kids at that age were smart enough to figure out if you brought a whole bunch in, they might stand a better chance going to Notre Dame or U. of D."

On the assigned night, Tobianski would drive the school bus to the homes of the prospects, pick them up, and shuttle them to St. Ambrose for the recruiting pitch.

"I guess it was legal," Boisture said, "or the league would have said something to us. They don't have NCAA rules regulating grade-school kids."

At first Boisture brought the kids to the school hall. Later, after the locker room was refurbished, he would stage his recruiting nights there to give the kids a better feel for what was in store for them as Ambrosians.

"We'd have a little party for them," Boisture said. "We brought them in and showed them what we had. We showed them our equipment. That was our pride and joy. We showed them our game films. We let some of our players talk to them, Bringard and people like that. The kids recruited for you. Jambor and that bunch did a helluva job selling the school."

Boisture had more to offer in 1957 than a chance to play for the defending East-side champions. There also was financial incentive for the kids. The Dad's Club would cover the tuition for the recruits. Back then, parish residents would pay $20 per family to attend St. Ambrose. Non-parish residents would pay $50 per family.

"That may not sound like a lot of money today," said Ray Malcoun, who attended grade school at St. Joan of Arc and was a member of the 1959 recruiting class. "But that was a lot of money at the time for my dad. He owned a small grocery business and had five kids to put through school. We all went to parochial schools. I had a sister at St. Paul, a brother at St. Bernard, another sister went to Regina and another younger brother coming up behind me. I'm sure that $50 was important."

So was that $20 to parishioners. Dave Brozo, a graduate of both St. Ambrose grade school and high school who would serve as a captain of the 1958 team, didn't think it was fair that kids from out of the parish were getting a better deal. So he took his complaint to the school's athletic director Fr. George Rozman.

"I want a break on tuition," Brozo said.

"It's only 20 bucks," Fr. Rozman said.

"Yeah," Brozo argued, "but you've got these other kids coming in who don't have to pay anything."

"Go to another school if you want," Fr. Rozman said.

End of conversation.

Photo courtesy Dave Vitali

Mike Cure

"I'm in their football system from fifth grade all the way up and I can't get a $20 break for my family," Brozo mused years later. "He was right — where was I going to go? Why would I want to go? If you were talking about an all-boys school, it would have cost a whole lot more than $20."

St. Ambrose did lose some parish kids to other schools. One would quarterback Southeastern against St. Ambrose in the 1964 Goodfellow Game. A few others would play for Notre Dame in Soup Bowls in the 1960s against St. Ambrose.

But Boisture wasn't going to allow the elite parish kids to leave in the 1950s. He drew the line with Mike Cure, a gifted multi-sport athlete at St. Ambrose grade school whose older brother Norm was already playing on the high-school team.

"Mike wanted to go to Austin to play basketball," Boisture recalled. "I talked him out of it. I told him he'd start in basketball and I'd give him a shot at quarterback."

Boisture told Cure he was going to take the basketball team to the next level along with the football team. The parish would build a new gymnasium — the school hall was barely large enough to stage grade-school games. There was only four feet of clearance all the way around the court. The cheerleaders performed on a stage at the one end of the court and the smattering of fans who attended the games would watch from a small balcony at the other end. The high school basketball team was forced to play its home games on the court of its bitter East-side rival Servite.

"That was the continuous argument," Norm Cure recalled. "Tom would say, 'We're going to knock that thing down and build a new gymnasium.' That was the technique he used to get my brother to St. Ambrose. He said, 'Mike, you c'mon over here and we're going to knock that thing down.' Then he'd tell me, 'Mike needs to come here, or your days of playing for St. Ambrose are over.'"

Mike Cure did elect to attend St. Ambrose High. He did play basketball and football, but graduated unfulfilled in both sports. St. Ambrose never did tear down the hall until both Cure and the school were long gone. It became a parking lot owned by the city of Grosse Pointe Park.

"Mike was not happy with me," Boisture said. "He thinks I screwed him. He thinks I lied to him. But I tried to get a basketball program going. We brought some kids in who could play — Goff, Fournier, Lantzy.... But I don't think the lot was big enough [for a new gymnasium]. The parish wanted something that would be used as more than just a gym."

In football, Mike Cure wound up playing just about every spot in the offensive backfield except quarterback. Boisture always found someone who fit the offense better at the position.

"Mike made a lot of mistakes," Boisture said, "but it may have been because I had him doing so many things. I had him punting, playing quarterback, then I moved him to fullback as a sophomore because we didn't have one. I probably did screw him up. I was never able to find the best position for him. I was always trying to get him to fill positions that I needed filled."

Boisture knew if he could keep the best parish kids and add a few elite players from St. Juliana, St. Veronica, and St. Joan of Arc, he could put St. Ambrose on Detroit's prep football map.

But there was one player Boisture knew he absolutely needed to win over in his first foray into recruiting in 1957 to move his program into the Catholic League's fast lane.

GRAMER

St. Joan of Arc wasn't an old parish by the Archdiocese of Detroit's standards. Founded in 1927, St. Joan of Arc was an infant compared to Redford St. Mary (1843), Holy Redeemer (1880), and Our Lady of Lourdes (1893).

The St. Joan grade school was even younger. The doors had been open for only 10 years when Tom Boisture first walked into the building to recruit the school's star player in 1957.

St. Joan didn't start playing football until 1955, but the Chargers became a fast force in CYO circles. They went from 0-8 in their inaugural season in 1955 to 5-2 in 1956. St. Joan also won the CYO baseball championship that season. Tony "Butch" Gramer was the catalyst for all that success.

"Gramer was the best football player, the best basketball player, the best baseball player," Boisture said. "He was the best athlete at St. Joan. Fullback, linebacker, offense, defense — you could play him anywhere you wanted. He's the one kid we really wanted."

But everyone else on the East side wanted Gramer, too. His older brother Russ was already on the football team at Notre Dame, and St. Joan of Arc was considered one of its feeder schools. In 1951, when the parish decided not to build a high school, St. Joan of Arc participated in the fundraising drive to build Notre Dame.

So Boisture strolled into St. Joan of Arc as an underdog in this recruiting battle. He needed an edge and quickly found one. He identified the camaraderie of that band of kids who played all three sports at St. Joan.

"We had a bunch of fun guys," Gramer said. "We also were a bunch of good athletes. We really tore it up. And we all lived close enough to ride our bikes to each other's homes."

So Boisture opened his recruiting net and pursued several of Gramer's teammates as well: Joe D'Angelo, Bill Fournier, and Dave Kulinski. Gramer caught, Fournier played second base, Kulinski third and D'Angelo centerfield for the St. Joan baseball team that swept Royal Oak Shrine, 1-0 and 9-0, in a best-of-three series for the CYO championship.

St. Ambrose was not even on their radar screen when Boisture invited the St. Joan Four to participate in one of his recruiting nights. But Boisture, Tobianski, and Fr. Rozman dazzled the St. Clair Shores grade schoolers.

D'Angelo was small, barely 135 pounds. He had been third fiddle in the St. Joan backfield to the bigger Gramer and faster Fournier, so high schools weren't knocking down his door. Before the St. Ambrose bus pulled up at his front door, D'Angelo figured he was headed to Notre Dame.

"When I was in seventh grade, Notre Dame was just opening up," D'Angelo said. "I thought, 'God, that's where I want to go.' To hear that fight song and everything... But St. Ambrose made sense — going to a school where it looked like I had a better chance to play. I wasn't that big. So a lot of us said, 'Let's go there.' It was almost like a group decision."

Fournier also was a quick convert.

"I never even heard of St. Ambrose," Fournier said. "It was just another school. I always figured I'd end up at Notre Dame because a lot of kids from St. Joan of Arc went there. Austin was too Grosse Pointey, and I wasn't into that kind of stuff. But the opportunity to go to St. Ambrose came along and it fit my needs.

"You have to realize a lot of our parents didn't have a whole lot of money. Notre Dame and Austin were expensive. What were your chances of playing there with all those kids? We wanted to play sports. So it didn't take much to talk you into going to St. Ambrose. It was a parochial school, which our parents wanted us to attend, and you'd have the opportunity to play more than one sport. If you went to Austin or Notre Dame, your chances of even playing one sport were going to be awfully slim. Nobody was going to know who we were."

Gramer would come to St. Ambrose as well — but not before he and his parents could cut a deal with Boisture.

"We told him as a condition you have to take the other three guys," Gramer said. "You've got to understand — we'd all been together since the fourth grade."

To get Gramer, the St. Ambrose Dad's Club needed to foot the tuition for three other St. Joan products. A fifth member of their clique, Jim LaRose, a pitcher on the St. Joan baseball team and a close friend and neighbor of D'Angelo, also would enroll at St. Ambrose. So would Gramer's brother Russ, who would transfer over from Notre Dame. Bill David, St. Joan's baseball coach, would be hired by St. Ambrose as its baseball coach and offensive backfield coach in football.

Only a player with swagger and ability could write his own ticket to St. Ambrose like Gramer. Boisture thought he was on his way after winning that recruiting battle — and he was. But not with Gramer. He suffered a knee injury in a scrimmage early in the fall of his freshman season.

"I continued to play on it even though it hurt," Gramer recalled. "I couldn't perform the way I wanted to. I think Tom was somewhat disappointed. I was, too, but I couldn't make excuses other than my knee hurt.

"At the end of the season they sent me to a doctor and he found out I had all this cartilage damage. They operated on me right away."

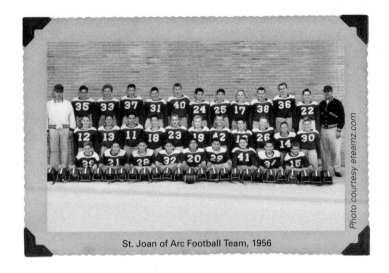

St. Joan of Arc Football Team, 1956

Photo courtesy eteamz.com

The St. Joan of Arc team included future St. Ambrose Cavaliers Joe D'Angelo (11), Bill Fournier (13), Ray Malcoun (20), Jim LaRose (22), Dave Kulinski (23), and Tony Gramer (38).

Gramer was a disappointment off the field as well.

"He got in trouble at the school, smarting off to the nuns," D'Angelo said.

Gramer lasted one year at St. Ambrose. He transferred to Notre Dame as a sophomore.

"We were a hell-raising bunch," said Gramer of the St. Joan brigade. "When you got us together, collectively, we were a pretty disruptive force. Then when you threw in the other guys we met that Boisture also recruited, it was, well…that was a long time ago. We had a lot of fun.

"We laughed a lot in the classroom and didn't pay much attention. I took the brunt of the disciplinary action. My brother got homesick and wanted to go back to Notre Dame, and their coach was knocking on the door pretty heavily to get me to go over there."

Gramer sat out the 1958 football season in the transfer, then his father took a job in Florida as a member of Wernher Von Braun's original NASA team in 1959. So the Gramers moved to Orlando, and Butch finished out his high-school career as a starting running back for Bishop Moore High School. He signed a baseball contract with the Cincinnati Reds out of high school.

But the Gramer deal was not one Boisture lived to regret. Fournier would become a four-sport letterman at St. Ambrose and win the Rozman Trophy in 1959-60 as the school's best all-around athlete. D'Angelo also would letter in four sports and win the Rozman Trophy as a senior in 1960-61.

Boisture didn't limit the scope of his recruiting class in 1957 to eighth graders, though.

10

CURRIE

The parents of Dave Brozo worked in factories, his dad at L.A. Young in Ferndale and his mom at Detroit Moulding in Ecorse. The two factories were owned by the same company, which sponsored a Sunday morning bowling league. Brozo's parents participated, as did Dave and a few friends in the summer of 1957.

Every Sunday morning after Mass, Brozo would drive over to Palace Lanes at Gratiot and East Grand Boulevard. He became friendly with a kid working the lunch counter named Mike Currie, who was a year younger than Brozo and played football for St. Anthony. Their friendship flourished and Brozo, who had been driving since he was 13, taught Currie how to drive his '49 Chevy that summer.

"I remember teaching him how to power shift," Brozo said, "and the gear shift spun right around the steering column. He slammed the gear shift so hard it broke."

The two got a chuckle over their Exorcist moment. Brozo was eager to tell Tom Boisture about his new friend.

"There's a kid I know over at bowling alley whose brother plays in the NFL for the Packers," Brozo told his coach. "Tom told me to do whatever I could to get him to come over to St. Ambrose."

The sticky part in this particular recruitment was that Mike was the younger brother of Dan Currie, the St. Anthony legend.

But Tom already knew about Mike Currie — and not because of that conversation with Brozo. And not because Currie was on the field in that 26-22 St. Anthony victory over St. Ambrose in

Mike Currie and Miles Currie

Photo courtesy Tom Boisture

1956. Boisture knew of Currie because one of his assistant coaches at St. Ambrose was Miles Currie, Mike's older brother.

Boisture knew that Mike's father was a fire captain on disability and his mother was an invalid. Boisture knew that money was tight in the Currie household. He also knew that Mike was not happy with his coach at St. Anthony.

"I told Miles to move his ass over here," Boisture said. "I told him we'd get the family a place."

So Brozo would spend his Sunday mornings selling Currie on the merits of attending school and playing football for St. Ambrose.

"It was hard for him because St. Anthony was a traditional power," Brozo said. "But we were coming up and they were going down.

And his neighborhood was going down some, too. I don't know if I ever convinced him to come. All I did was encourage him."

Come August, the Currie family was ready to move into Grosse Pointe Park.

"Tobianski found the family a place," Boisture said. "It was a flat right down the street from John. Miles and I went over and moved them ourselves — the furniture, everything. Whenever they couldn't meet rent, we took care of that. That wasn't a problem. That's what the parish does — it helps people who are in need."

And Boisture was in need of another stud on his defense.

11

SETTING THE TABLE

There was optimism heading into the 1957 season based on past performance. St. Ambrose had come within a game of playing for a city championship in 1956, and there was anxiety in the parish to take the next step.

But reality was about to author a different script. The Cavaliers were a senior-laden team in 1956. Now Jambor, Lloyd Bayer, Don Benvenuti, Bill Krause, Mike Taormino, Chuck Valdez, and that talented crew had all graduated. Inexperience abounded in 1957. There was a new quarterback in Mike Ward and only a handful of seniors.

Tom Boisture wasn't sure what to expect from his second St. Ambrose entry. But he was pleasantly surprised two Sundays into the season when his Cavaliers sat 2-0 with shutout victories over Mount Clemens St. Mary and St. Stanislaus. Maybe this team did have the savvy to go back to the Soup Bowl.

Then again, maybe not.

The Cavaliers were hit with a spate of Asiatic flu in October, depleting the ranks. Over the next three weekends St. Ambrose tied Servite 6-6 and was paddled by St. Catherine, 31-0, and St. Anthony, 32-13. Ward collapsed on the field in the St. Anthony game and spent the next three weeks in the hospital with double pneumonia. His season was over.

The Cavaliers were scuffling along at 2-2-1. There would be no return to the Soup Bowl. If there was no present for his team, Boisture decided he needed to start building a future. So he put his freshmen on the field.

Photo courtesy Dave Vitali

Bill Fournier

Manny Lamprides took over at quarterback. Joe D'Angelo and Bill Fournier also hit the field. So did a couple of parish kids, Larry Lantzy and Skip Paoletti. Boisture was waving the white flag.

"Tom figured if this team was going to get any better, he needed to start playing the underclassmen," said Gerry Stogniew, one of the seniors. "And he did. In hindsight, he was right. We weren't as good as we thought we were. When we played a good team, they beat us up pretty bad."

The three freshman running backs — D'Angelo, Fournier, and Lantzy — all lettered that season. So did Lamprides and lineman Dave Kulinski, the least of the St. Joan Four.

Even with youth on the field, St. Ambrose was competitive, beating St. Ladislaus 13-6 and playing St. Florian to a scoreless tie in the finale. A 3-2-2 season was quite a letdown from that Soup Bowl experience in 1956, but Boisture found reason for encouragement.

First, junior guard Larry Bringard was emerging as a leader on and off the field. He was spending every waking hour at the school lifting weights — decades before weight-training became vogue at any level of football, much less high school. He wanted to become bigger, stronger, and better, and saw a set of barbells as his way to achieve that goal. So Boisture had Tobianski set up a small room off the shower for lifting weights.

"After that season, we got them all on the weights," Boisture said. "I didn't have any big guys. I felt we needed to build some of those young linemen up."

Secondly, the snapshot Lamprides provided at the end of the 1957 season convinced Boisture he had the quarterback in place to take him to another Soup Bowl. Boisture threw the ball because he had Jambor in 1956. Now he needed to find an offense to feature the strengths of Lamprides, who was a ball-handler extraordinaire.

Boisture went to his football library and started reading up on offenses. A book written by Delaware coach and University of Michigan alumnus Davey Nelson on the Wing T, "Scoring Power with the Winged-T Offense" (written with University of Michigan quarterback Forest Evashevski) intrigued him.

"I studied and studied and studied that book," Boisture said.

When he felt he had a grasp of the offense, Boisture called Jerry Burns, a defensive assistant at the University of Iowa. He had been the pre-Dan Boisture head coach at Redford St. Mary in 1953, and Boisture came to know Burns when he returned to Detroit to recruit Hamtramck. Iowa implemented the Wing T in 1956 and won both the Big Ten title and Rose Bowl. Burns, who would become the head coach of the Minnesota Vikings later in life after gaining a reputation as an offensive guru, could give Boisture a defensive perspective on the offense.

The offense was a cross between a T-formation and single wing, in that there was always a wingback lined up to the right or left. The wingback always went into motion and the quarterback might offer up two or three handoffs during a single play. The offense was built on misdirection and pulling guards. That brought into play Boisture's best player — Bringard.

With the fast feet of D'Angelo, Fournier, and Lantzy, the fast hands of Lamprides and the agile Bringard out front blocking, Boisture believed he could stage a fire drill on every play.

"The quarterback had to slip the ball in here, keep a hand in there, ride this guy," said Boisture, all the while gesturing with his hands as if he was dealing cards in a Las Vegas casino. "Lamprides wasn't fast but he could hide the ball and keep right on running. He could keep it on the bootleg. This was an offense built for him."

So Boisture was more excited about 1958 than the 1957 season when he was defending the East-side championship. The 1958 season wasn't going to be about defending anything — it was going to be about winning everything.

But Fr. George Rozman would not be around to see the mission completed. He was having heart problems and accepted a transfer out of St. Ambrose in 1957. Before Fr. Rozman departed, he poured more of the Dad's Club money into starting a hockey team at the school. The coach? The versatile janitor, John Tobianski. It was a final going-away present from Fr. Rozman. Hockey would become another recruiting tool for the Cavaliers.

Fr. William Pettit replaced Fr. Rozman as the school's athletic director.

UNIFORMS

The Catholic League wouldn't recognize the St. Ambrose Cavaliers in 1958. The Cavaliers would hardly recognize themselves.

The Dad's Club was flush with cash. It staged weekly 50-50 raffles, with the winner claiming half the pot with the Dad's Club keeping the other half. The Dad's Club made it easy for parishioners to participate in the fundraising, setting up card tables at the back of the church to sell the tickets after Sunday Mass. It became the St. Ambrose way — donate to the pagan babies during Mass and give to the football team afterwards.

"They raised a tremendous amount of money," Joe D'Angelo said. "There was one guy in the Dad's Club who owned a fruit market and would sell 500-1,000 tickets on his own."

In 1958, after a few years of raffles and paper drives, the Dad's Club was anxious to start spending. The lads would be outfitted in new uniforms, head to toe. The Cavaliers would no longer look like St. Anthony, who shared the same maroon and white color scheme. The Cavaliers would look like the Detroit Lions.

"My understanding was it was the same equipment the pros were wearing — silk-type pants, a rayon jersey," center Ray Federspiel said. "The pants were bright white. They came in and measured everyone for helmets with numbers on the sides, really nice stuff."

The running backs were given girdles to hold the pads. No longer would they have to insert their own pads into slots in the pants. The pants were spandex when everyone else in the high school game was wearing cloth.

St. Ambrose Athletic Association (a.k.a. The Dad's Club)

Photo courtesy Dave Brozo/Gari Michaels

"Our uniforms were mesh and lightweight," defensive back Pete Piazza said. "The pants, the cleats — everything we had was first class. Our uniforms were classy. But the helmets topped it off."

St. Ambrose went to the Riddell fiberglass suspension helmets in 1958. The elastic crown inside the helmet provided an air cushion to absorb contact by the head. It was the newest, safest, best product on the market.

"There were colleges that didn't have Riddell helmets back then," guard Bill Lenhard said. "There were pro teams that didn't have our suspension helmets. They were still using the full-pad helmets."

Boisture decided to give the helmets some flair. He wanted a look that would set St. Ambrose apart from the rest — a look that commanded respect the moment the Cavaliers burst onto the football field.

The Cavaliers had worn maroon helmets in the early to mid 1950s with a wide white stripe. When Boisture arrived in 1956, he put one thin stripe down the middle of the helmet. But in 1958 Boisture made a fashion statement. He put three stripes on the helmet — just like the University of Michigan.

The Wolverines enjoyed almost a century of football success under coaches Fielding Yost, Fritz Crisler, and Bennie Oosterbaan. Michigan built itself into a perennial Big Ten power that was easily identifiable every Saturday by those three yellow stripes atop the blue helmets.

Boisture wanted that same identification for his Cavaliers on Friday nights with those three white stripes atop the maroon helmets.

The new look wasn't completely the product of Dad's Club money, however. One of Boisture's assistants was Jim Louwers, whose older brother Jay was a sales representative for Griswold's Sporting Goods. Jay developed a quick affection for St. Ambrose.

"I got to know him really well," Boisture said. "He was a heck of a guy and was around all the time. We did all of our buying from Jay. He got us the Michigan helmets and made sure we always had the latest and best equipment."

Like shoulder pads.

"I remember when they came out with the fiberglass shoulder pads," Lenhard said. "Jay Louwers brings them in, I put them on and Tobianski is hitting me on the shoulders with a baseball bat. Jay said, 'Go ahead, give him a whack.'"

As the winning increased over the years, the investment in equipment would increase. Ray Malcoun would go on to play college ball at the University of Detroit and Drake.

"They weren't big programs," Malcoun said, "but they were still college programs. The equipment we had at St. Ambrose was head and shoulders above anything I had in college. I had game shoes and practice shoes. And they were always polished. I didn't know who was polishing them, but they were always polished. It was a top-notch program. It was unbelievable what we had."

Marshall Houle would go on from St. Ambrose to play at Wyoming. Mike Goff went on to play his college ball at Buffalo. Same story — they wore better equipment in high school than in college.

Tom Beer said his high-school equipment was on a par with what he wore with the Boston Patriots in 1970.

"There wasn't a team within 100 miles of us that was as spoiled as we were," added Piazza. "All you needed to do was show up. Everything else was provided for you. If you cracked your shoulder pads, they'd replace them in an instant. Crack your helmet…new.

"I got whacked around the end of my junior year and suffered some concussions. My mom and dad were concerned. Our doctor advised me not to play football my senior year in case I got hit again. So the school bought me a helmet with double padding throughout and all these whistles and bells and told me, 'This is as safe as you can ever be. It will protect you three times better than any helmet.' The school assured my parents I'd be O.K. It worked — (40-plus years later) I can still count and talk in complete sentences. Anything you needed or wanted at St. Ambrose was yours."

D'Angelo remembers getting a new pair of soft, kangaroo leather shoes every season. Lightweight shoes made a running back feel faster, and kangaroo was the emerging material of choice in the late 1950s. Over the years the shoes became more plentiful.

"They used to put me in new kangaroo leather shoes every week," said Pete Genord, who graduated in 1963.

"My senior year I had three different pair of shoes," said Mike VanGoethem, a classmate of Genord. "Those don't feel right? Here, try these…."

The uniforms weren't the only subject of a makeover in 1958. Tobianski put together a crew that would expand and enhance the locker room in the basement of the school. One of the casualties was the sewing classroom, which was swallowed up by the football program. Space was set aside for a training room and equipment room and each player would have his own cubicle. Tobianski also installed a ventilation system in each individual locker that would dry out the equipment after use. That came in especially handy during those steamy two-a-days of August.

Practicing in the new maroon uniforms, 1959

Detroit Free Press photo courtesy Tom Boisure

"We went from putting our pants on a hook to having your own locker with your name on it," offensive lineman Skip Paoletti said. "It was a tremendous thing playing football for St. Ambrose. All you had to do is show up naked and they'd give you everything you'd need — socks, shoes, shirt, short, towels, equipment, a locker."

The showers remained across the hallway in the boys' bathroom. But there were metal fences with curtains that could be drawn after practice to partition the locker/shower area off from the rest of the school — and from the rest of the outside world, for that matter.

"The locker room had its own aura," D'Angelo said. "We felt like we were special. We were downstairs in the dungeon. The coaches had their inner sanctum. It was a special little room. At lunchtime we didn't mingle with the other kids. We went down there and watched film. We'd sit on our benches and eat our lunch.

"I'm sure there were some people who thought we were elitists, even among our own little group. But you didn't have what you had in other schools, the competition from other sports. The other sports at St. Ambrose were mostly football players anyway. I played basketball, track, and hockey."

St. Ambrose also was way ahead of its time in the treatment of injuries. The Cavaliers were the only school on the East side with a whirlpool. Tobianski made it available to injured players from other schools, parochial and public, and they would make a trek to Hampton Road to sit in the St. Ambrose tub. The Dad's Club contracted a chiropractor to work out the kinks in players and also provided ultra-sound treatments for running backs suffering from deep thigh bruises or hamstring issues.

"We had the best equipment, the best medical care, the best of everything," said linebacker Dave Brozo, the captain of the 1958 team.

The Cavaliers were put into position to succeed. For that, they could thank the Dad's Club, which had bankrolled the transformation of St. Ambrose into a first-class program.

"The Dad's Club had gobs of money," Boisture said. "Anything that was old, John would throw away. We bought whatever we wanted, whatever we needed."

BOISTURE

The 1958 Cavaliers were starting to adopt the personality of their coach.

Two recruiting classes allowed Tom Boisture to inject his type of athlete into the St. Ambrose roster. Speed was more important to Boisture than size. He also was able to start collecting players sharing his work ethic and toughness.

Even though Boisture inherited Larry Bringard and Dave Brozo upon his arrival in 1956, he considered them his type of players. That's why he designated them as co-captains in 1958. Whether it was Bringard pumping iron hour-after-hour in a makeshift weight room or Brozo recruiting future teammates in a bowling alley, the two seniors were prepared to take whatever steps necessary to avoid a repeat of the 1957 season.

"They took over that team," Boisture said. "They would walk through fire if I told them."

Bringard proved that in August. Looking for any edge he could find on the field, Boisture had John Tobianski nail a 2x4 to the wall near the shower for the offensive linemen to work on their hand punch.

"Shit, Tom, they'll break their hands," Tobianski said.

"No they won't," Boisture scoffed. "It will toughen them up."

So Bringard would religiously troop the linemen to that 2x4 on a daily basis and they'd go down the line punching the wooden board with bare knuckles.

"They'd hit it full speed not knowing they had to open up their hands," Boisture said. "But it didn't faze them. They figured, 'If this is what we have to do to win....' They swallowed it hook, line and sinker.

"They're hitting that damn thing and getting all skinned up. So I finally told them, 'Now that you've got your knuckles all toughened up, hit it with your (open) hands.' Tobianski came in and told me, 'If we don't put a pad on that board, you're going to kill them.' I tell you what — that was a tough bunch. But we did put a pad up the next year."

Freshman guard Bill Lenhard found out just how tough a bunch it was in the opening session of two-a-days that August. After one day, Lenhard knew one thing about St. Ambrose football — he wanted no part it.

"I took the worst beating of my life," Lenhard said. "Boisture put me with Bringard and Jerry Palazzola in drills. I'm a freshman, Jerry is a sophomore and Larry [Bringard] is Larry. Bringard busted my facemask right off, busted my nose. I went through the entire double session with a broken nose. To this day I've never taken a beating like that.

"I went home and said, 'I'm through. I just can't do this.' But before I got home, Boisture had called my dad and told him, 'Bill's going to come home and want to quit. Don't let him. He's going to be a helluva football player.' My dad didn't tell me that until several years later."

Lenhard did stick it out. In 1961, he became the school's second All-America.

Jim Dinverno was another newcomer to the Cavaliers in 1958. He transferred to St. Ambrose, coming over from Nativity. But unlike Mike Currie, Dinverno already lived in the parish. He grew up near Harper and Van Dyke in the Nativity parish, where he attended grade school. But with Jim about to enter high school, the Dinvernos moved to Nottingham in Grosse Pointe Park in 1957.

Nativity was a Second Division power, finishing 6-2 in 1956.

All of his childhood friends were going to attend Nativity, so Dinverno decided he would continue his education there despite his departure from the parish. He spent his freshman season as a 145-pound backup linebacker, taking the bus back and forth to school each day. Nativity again finished 6-2.

"The bussing was a pain," Dinverno said, "so I finally switched to St. Ambrose for my sophomore year."

That decision made life easier for Dinverno as a student. Now his high school was only six blocks away. It also made his life considerably easier as a football player. St. Ambrose practiced across the street at Defer.

So Dinverno was welcomed with open arms by his new teammates. The Cavaliers quickly came to appreciate the unique location of his home during his tenure as their teammate.

"They never let us have any water," Tom Beer said. "So after practice we'd run across the street to Jim Dinverno's house and drink water out of his garden hose. We'd fill our helmets full of water."

The lack of water on the practice field was one of the training quirks of Tobianski, who had no formal medical background yet served as the team trainer. There were water bottles available, but no one dared drink from them.

"Tobianski would put dishwasher soap in the drinking water so you wouldn't swallow it," Bill Fournier said. "He said back then that drinking water would give you cramps. So you'd rinse your mouth out but never swallow it."

Tobianski also had a novel way of treating bumps and bruises.

"He'd tell us to rub a little dirt on it," Mike Goff said.

Tobianski had a novel way of treating lots of ailments as the team trainer.

"One time I had a sore throat during a game," Skip Paoletti said. "I was feeling kind of puke. So Tobianski comes over and asks me, 'Skip, what's the problem?' I told him I was having problems swallowing. He said, 'No problem. Come over here, son.' He pulled out a tongue depressor and scooped out about a quarter pound of analgesic balm, put it on my tongue and told me to swallow it.

"To this day every time I take a Hall's mentholyptus [cough drop] I think of that."

But with anything more serious than a sore throat or a thigh bruise, the players learned they'd better get a second opinion.

"He thought he was a medical doctor," Piazza said.

He wasn't.

"He didn't coddle people," Brozo said. "When I broke my ankle my junior year, he kept saying, 'There's nothing wrong with you. Don't be such a baby.' I said, 'John, it's broken. I heard it snap. I know it's broken.' He said, 'Naw, it's not broken. Get tough.'

"So I walked home that night. I also walked up to the White Tower and back home again. But everything hurt so much that I drove myself over to Bon Secours Hospital, where the doctor confirmed my ankle was broken. The next day I went to school with my leg in a cast. That ended my junior season. Tobianski never said a word to me about it. He just looked the other way. He wasn't a doctor. He botched that one."

With Boisture as their coach and Tobianski their trainer, the Cavaliers had no choice but to be tough. And disciplined.

Boisture was a stickler for details. In the Wing T, he found an offense that would be with him the rest of his days at St. Ambrose. It was a finesse scheme based on precision and timing. St. Ambrose would need perfect execution to defeat opponents who on a weekly basis would be bigger and stronger than the Cavaliers.

Boisture made his expectations perfectly clear in the 16-page mimeographed handout he gave the players when they reported for two-a-days that summer. It would serve as their playbook, although only the last four pages would include diagrams of any plays.

The handout was entitled, "ESSENTIALS FOR A GREAT

Photo courtesy Dave Vitali

Tom Boisture

FOOTBALL TEAM." The capitalization was to reinforce his goal — greatness. Throughout the first 12 pages were tips on how to maximize performance — keep your feet moving, always play at full speed, football takes brains. A few key sentences were capitalized:

```
IF YOU PLAY YOUR FOOTBALL RIGHT,
YOU CAN WIN, EVEN FROM GOOD OPPONENTS.

A TEAM THAT DOES NOT MAKE MISTAKES
RARELY LOSES A FOOTBALL GAME.
```

So Boisture drilled perfection on the practice field. No mistakes — not even on Tuesday at Defer when no one was keeping score and the snaps didn't count. Practice makes perfect. It became tedious and monotonous at times for the players.

"Boisture would have us run the same play over and over and over again until we got it right," Ray Malcoun said. "As the fullback I was supposed to line up directly behind the center and quarterback. If I wasn't, Boisture would come and knock me over before we started the play. He was always concerned that if I was lined up a little to the right or a little to the left I'd be tipping off the play. He was a perfectionist — and they drilled us to perfection."

Boisture was as demanding of his linemen as he was his backs. He would regularly station Tobianski or a coach on the sideline at the line of scrimmage to make sure the blockers were perfectly straight. In a three-point stance, Boisture wanted all helmets aligned at the back point of the football. Correct foot placement, correct hand placement, correct helmet placement — Boisture was of the belief if a play didn't start out perfect it could never finish perfect.

Once he got his line perfect, Boisture became even more finicky with his ball carriers.

"His theory was when you hit the hole, wherever it was, your shoulders had to be square," Brozo said. "He wouldn't let you hit the hole at an angle like they do now. You had to plant and get your shoulders square through the hole or you were going to run the play again. Even if you saw no hole, you had to hit up in there square behind the block. He was a stickler for that. I think that's why we ran such an effective offense."

The perfection and, of course, the misdirection. Backs would be heading off in all directions at the snap in the Wing T. Manny Lamprides might offer up a handoff to the fullback on an apparent plunge, then pull the ball back and pitch it to the wingback zipping by. Sometimes Lamprides would hand the ball to the halfback, who would in turn hand it off to the wingback. Double- and triple-reverses weren't gimmicks in the St. Ambrose offense. They were staples.

"There was a lot of deception," Larry Lantzy said. "There were guys going in three directions — the wingback would be going one way, the halfback the other and the fullback up the middle. We'd catch everyone by surprise. People had a hard time defending us."

But all the deception wasn't on the field. There was some on the St. Ambrose sideline as well.

PLAYOFF

Jim Louwers was a senior attending the University of Detroit in 1958 and drew St. Ambrose as his student teaching assignment. He looked young enough to be one of the students himself.

But Louwers did more than attend school in his first two years at U. of D. He also served as an assistant offensive football coach at Grosse Pointe St. Paul High School. So when Louwers was assigned to teach Algebra at St. Ambrose, Tom Boisture offered him the chance to be help coach his football team.

Boisture put Louwers to work on the practice field at Defer — and a few other practice fields around the east side of town.

"I used to take my girlfriend — later my wife — to some practices of our opponents," Louwers said. "We'd be dating, walking around and necking. So we were standing on the sideline watching a St. Florian practice one day and the coach came over and asked me what I was doing. I told him I went to the University of Detroit and was interested in becoming a coach — all of which was true.

"So he takes me onto the field, right into their huddle, and tells me, 'Do you want to see something neat? This is what we're going to do against St. Ambrose this week.' They were going to let some St. Ambrose linemen through and then trap block them. I went back and told Boisture. He made the necessary adjustments."

St. Ambrose smoked St. Florian, 25-6, in the 1958 season opener.

Coaches weren't allowed on the field during timeouts in games. A captain could come to the sideline to talk to the coaches, but the rest of the team would have to wait for those instructions. Again, St. Ambrose would benefit from having a boyish assistant.

"I would take the water bucket out and tell everyone what the coaches wanted them to do," Louwers said. "To be able to go on the field and talk to the players gave us an advantage. Everyone thought I was a senior. Boisture knew all the angles, and it paid off."

The second game was a big one for Louwers — St. Paul. The Lakers were making the step up from Second Division to First in Catholic League play in 1958. This would be their first game against their Grosse Pointe neighbor St. Ambrose. The Cavaliers expected to trounce the Lakers.

"Boisture told us when we go out to the field, instead of screaming and yelling, come out silent as you trot around the field and line up for drills," Dave Brozo said. "He said that would scare the crap out of them. Well, it had the opposite effect. They got the idea we were overconfident and wound up playing the best game they ever played against us. We were lucky."

St. Ambrose would prevail, 13-12. The Lakers would never again play the Cavaliers that close in football.

That fall Boisture was carving out an edge in the classroom as well. He taught drafting at St. Ambrose, and the makeover of the locker room provided him a classroom off the back of the coal bin that served as his office. Drafting became Football 101, a staple for all of his players.

"During drafting class Bringard and I would go into the coaches' office with Boisture and watch game film," Brozo said. "I'm sure all the other teams were doing the same thing. I didn't do a drafting project that whole year and got a B+."

The Wing T was starting to take off as sophomores D'Angelo, Fournier, and Lantzy began flashing their speed. They were able to thrive because a small senior class was able to subjugate its ego.

"Boisture called Bringard and I in and said you guys are going to have to sacrifice because these young kids don't know how to block,"

Brozo recalled. "He told me he could let me run the ball — but I wouldn't have anyone blocking for me. So he asked me, 'What do you want to do for the team?' I told him I'd do whatever he wanted me to do. It didn't matter to me. I liked blocking anyway."

Larry Lantzy's 96-yard touchdown gallop highlighted St. Ambrose's 32-0 romp over St. Stanislaus, and the Cavaliers crushed rival Servite, 39-20. Then came the defining two games of the season — St. Catherine and St. Anthony.

Not only was St. Catherine was the defending Catholic East champion, the Warriors were the No. 1 ranked team in Class C and brought a 4-0 record into the St. Ambrose game, outscoring the opposition 163-19 along the way. But the Cavaliers prevailed, 13-7, when Manny Lamprides threw a touchdown pass to Mike Currie and ran for another score.

Buoyed by that upset, St. Ambrose steamrolled St. Anthony, 38-12, behind fullback Jim Laskowski's three touchdowns. It was the first time the Cavaliers had beaten the mighty Teutons since their arrival in the First Division, snapping a string of four consecutive defeats, and the Cavaliers went on to capture the East with a 6-0 record.

The Catholic League was divided up in three sectors — East, Central, and West. On a rotating basis, one geographical champion would draw a bye into the Soup Bowl and the other two would stage a play-in game. The Cavaliers drew the play-in game against Central champ the University of Detroit High, which was making the switch from the Detroit Public School League to the Catholic League that season. The winner would earn a Soup Bowl engagement with West champion Redford St. Mary.

Boisture was salivating at the prospect. An eighth victory over U. of D. would give him the chance to coach against his brother Dan for the first time. But this was a young St. Ambrose team with only four seniors in the starting lineup — and this wasn't going to be their night. The Cubs recovered three fumbles in the St. Am-

St. Ambrose defense against Servite, 1958

Photo courtesy John Dziurman

brose end and converted them all into touchdowns for a 20-7 triumph over the Cavaliers.

For the second time in three seasons under Boisture, St. Ambrose came up a game short. But Norm Cure had the sense better days were ahead at the little Catholic school on the East side.

"Jay Louwers was always around," Cure said, "and all of a sudden we had all these other people hanging around. The Michigan Catholic would come over and interview Larry [Bringard]. They'd come over to talk to Mike Currie. You knew something was going on. You knew there was a foundation there for success. But I had no idea it was going to become what it became."

In November, Lamprides was named All-East side quarterback. In December, Bringard became the school's first All-America. Five days after that loss to U. of D., St. Ambrose opened the basketball season against Catholic League power St. Paul and their legendary coach Ed Lauer.

"We had all football players — Currie, Cure, Lamprides — and we had only four days of practice," Boisture said. "Those bastards had been practicing for a month. They kicked the crap out of us at their place, doubling our score.

"After the game I met Eddie right in the middle of the fricking floor and said, 'Eddie, that was rotten. You humiliated these kids. I'll get you for this. You better wear two pairs of pants for that first football game because I'm going to kick your ass. I'll get you.'

"I went in that locker room and told those kids that was not fair to them as athletes and that I'd never think of doing that to them under the same circumstances. I told them to remember this — all you guys play football. We'll get those sons of bitches back. We'll triple the score on them."

St. Ambrose would settle all scores in 1959.

15

HALL

The playoff loss to University of Detroit High did little to slow the momentum Tom Boisture was building on Hampton Road.

The St. Ambrose Cavaliers compiled a 16-5-2 record in Boisture's first three seasons, finishing a victory away from of the Goodfellow Game in 1956 and a victory away from the Soup Bowl in 1958. Grade school kids on the east side were taking notice.

Boisture followed up the 1958 season with his best recruiting class yet. Mike Goff would come over from St. Veronica in 1959, as would Ray Malcoun and Cory Richardson from St. Joan of Arc. Tom Beer, Pete Genord and Chuck Kuess would come in from St. Matthew. Marshall Houle and Pete Piazza, like all good parishioners, opted to stay home to continue their schooling at St. Ambrose.

"When we started winning, it was like shooting fish in a barrel," Boisture said. "They all wanted to come. We had a lock on St. Veronica, a lock on St. Joan of Arc."

So Boisture started exploring new markets. St. Joan of Arc was pushing his recruiting envelope a bit in St. Clair Shores. It was located just north of Eight Mile Road. But Boisture burrowed even deeper into St. Clair Shores in 1959, tapping St. Isaac Jogues off 10 Mile Road.

St. Isaac Jogues had only been a parish since 1954. The school had only been open for two years and didn't even have a football team. But Boisture had been in the school's gymnasium as a basketball referee and so had his assistant, Bill David. They knew Ron Albers was an athlete.

"We were at basketball practice one day and Tom came over to talk to me," Albers said. "He asked if I was interested in attending a parochial high school with a football program. I hadn't even thought about high school. I figured I'd attend [St. Clair Shores] Lakeview."

Albers became an easy sell. Fellow eight-grader Mike Van Goethem didn't play basketball at Jogues. But he did play city league football with Albers for the Black Knights. He became a throw in.

"There really wasn't a recruitment process," Van Goethem said. "A couple of fathers in the [St. Ambrose] Dad's Club were in our parish, so they recruited Ron and myself."

Boisture was anxious to get all of his new players in uniform. They would make the Cavaliers a deeper, more talented team. But Boisture would have to wait until the fall for them. He would not have to wait to get his returning players in uniform, however.

Boisture was in the process of turning football into a year-round endeavor at St. Ambrose. But in the eight months the Cavaliers were not visible to public eyes they were still visible to Boisture's eyes — in the school's hall.

"We'd start in January and go all winter and spring," Joe D'Angelo said. "It was half-live. We'd wear pads but not pants. It was live in the line. You ran and made contact but you didn't tackle. We scrimmaged Hamtramck in the gym. I think we played Salesian there as well."

Boisture did not bother inquiring with the Catholic League about the legality of such practices. Why invite trouble? He'd lock the hall doors from the inside and cover all the windows with curtains, paint, boards or newspapers. He himself enjoyed freedom of movement. He could enter the hall through the tunnel beneath the street. So no one could see Boisture — and no one could see his football team.

Photo courtesy Jim Conahan

1959 St. Ambrose team - offense

Top row: Gil Otts, Mike Currie; 2nd row: Jim Conahan, Jerry Palazzola, Ray Federspiel; 3rd row: Manny Lamprides, Jack Cairo, Henry Babisz, Joe D'Angelo; Bottom row: Larry Lantzy, Vince Taormino.
Photo by Detroit News

The hall itself was a bandbox, barely large enough to contain a basketball court. Wooden benches and wrought iron steam radiators lined the walls on two sides. Padding? Not likely. Run a sweep and you might get thrown head first into a radiator. There also was no air conditioning. In July, it would be a billion degrees in the hall. Or so it seemed to a bunch of teenagers wearing football gear.

"The windows were shut," Dave Vitali said. "The doors were shut. There was no air coming in. You were sweating like fools. And we're there in full equipment going live."

The hall originally was the parish church. St. Ambrose parishioners worshipped there for 11 years, from 1917-27, before the new church was built on Hampton. But the only religion being practiced there in 1959 was football.

"Look around today," said Skip Paoletti decades later. "Schools are spending millions of dollars to build these huge indoor facilities — and we had one back then over at the hall. We were playing arena football long before anyone ever came up with the idea. We did a lot of things that were probably not allowed at the time. But we did them anyway."

Bill Lenhard had a different perspective on the indoor practices from D'Angelo. He had a lineman's perspective.

"We were working in full pads," Lenhard said. "It was full speed contact. I remember one drill with a center, guard and me. They had a guy standing at tackle. I'd practice doing a pull and taking him out. We used to do it with a high jump bar. They'd keep lowering the bar and you had to keep clearing it. If you touched the bar, you were going to run [laps]. There was a pivot point and you had to stay low.

"So Tom decides to have (captain) Jim Conahan stand over at tackle. He was strong. Conahan told me about it later. We went one-on-one on a hardwood floor. Conahan was punishing me. When you know the guard is coming on a trap, you can clobber him. Tom walked by Conahan and say, 'Hit him harder.' I had blood running down my face. It was bone-on-bone. Shorts, shoulder pads and helmet, full-speed contact. Jack Cairo was going to be the next guy up and he's thinking, 'I don't want to do this.' There was blood on the floor. My blood. Tom was relentless getting his point across."

That was the sense of urgency in which Boisture would approach the 1959 season. He viewed this as his best team yet with 10 returning starters on an offense that averaged 24 points per game in 1958. Boisture wanted to ensure his players would be ready for the challenge that awaited them. So he squeezed in a few extra practices.

The freshman would have to wait until August to participate. Little did they know what fun was in store for them.

16

SLAVES

There were four classes of players at St. Ambrose in the 1950s — seniors, juniors, sophomores and slaves.

It was a rite of passage. The hotshot eighth-grade recruits would enroll at St. Ambrose in the fall brimming with hopes and aspirations. Then the upper classmen would proceed to batter their spirit with demeaning tasks.

"You had to pay your dues," Joe D'Angelo said. "I remember riding the bus as a freshman. The seniors sat in the back and would call a freshman back there. There was some hazing going on. We'd have to carry their uniforms and clean their shoes.

"But we were cocky, even as freshmen. I remember we had a freshman night where we all had to learn songs. We started singing the songs and injecting the names of seniors, making fun of them. They ripped us up after that pretty good, just to remind us who was the boss."

Dave Brozo thought he succeeded in abolishing slavery at St. Ambrose when he became the team captain in 1958.

"I didn't allow it," Brozo said. "With only six seniors, how are you going to have slaves? I thought we were all supposed to be helping each other. Then I came to find out [fellow co-captain Larry] Bringard had his own slave and I didn't even know it."

On the first day of two-a-days, the upperclassmen would draft their slaves. The seniors got first crack. In 1959, captain Jim Conahan claimed Ray Malcoun. Fellow captain Vince Taormino selected Mike Goff. Linebacker Mike Currie took Marshall Houle and guard Jerry Palazzola snagged Mike Van Goethem. One-by-one the freshman were plucked like apples off a tree.

Boisture and his staff closed their eyes to the shenanigans. Don't ask, don't tell.

"Boisture was of the opinion if you're winning games and there's a little harassment, who cares?" Pete Piazza said. "As long as it didn't get out of hand — someone getting hurt or breaking a leg. But it never reached that point. They [seniors] told us don't ever let the coaches see the welts on your bottom after you've been initiated in the room. It was all part of the game."

Some of the slave work was routine.

"You had to carry their equipment, polish their shoes, change their cleats, hand them the soap, get them a towel," Goff said.

Some of the slave work was anything but routine.

"There was a lot of harassment, torment, physical pain," Piazza said. "Some guys would make it brutal. Some guys would take advantage of it. It was unbelievable some of the things that were done. Not to maim anybody, but just harassment."

And humiliation. The upperclassmen would spit at the freshman. The frosh would be jostled, pushed, and punched. Races would be staged in the shower, where slaves would have to push bars of soap with their noses across the slippery wet floor. Freshmen would be packed into a 55-gallon drum and rolled down the stone stairways inside the school.

"There wasn't anything I went through that I recall as being bad," Malcoun said. "But I'm sure there are some stories out there about Lantzy and whoever his freshman was."

That would be Larry Lantzy, the starting wingback. He may have been the fastest player ever to suit up for St. Ambrose. His speed would attract a football scholarship from the University of Houston. But that wouldn't come until 1961. He couldn't leave town fast enough for the freshman class of 1959. Lantzy made every freshman his slave.

"He was just an ornery bastard — always," Van Goethem said. "He'd be the guy you'd want on your side in a street fight. But he was a real pain in the ass. There were times we'd talk about getting three of us together and whipping his ass."

Boisture was hard on his football team. Lantzy was harder.

"The practices never got to me, but the hazing did," Tom Beer said. "They were obnoxious, and Lantzy would continue to harass the sophomores. He was a real pisser.

"But he really hated Servite, and in my sophomore year I started that game at defensive end. Bill Kemp faded back to pass, put his arm up, I hit him, he fumbled and we recovered and scored. After that play, Larry was my best friend."

Beer was recruited from St. Matthew along with Pete Genord and Chuck Kuess. Genord actually was headed to St. Anthony until he discovered St. Ambrose had a hockey team. But he lasted longer in hockey as a freshman than he did in football. Genord quit football after a week.

"It was too much of a hassle carrying all the seniors' equipment back to the gym, polishing their shoes and all that," Genord said. "I said, 'Are you crazy?' I knew some of the upper classmen from my neighborhood and told them, 'Naw, I'm not going to do that.' The senior football players who also played hockey — Conahan and Ray DeVriendt — asked me, 'What are you going to do, quit hockey, too?'

"But back then I was one of their better hockey players so I got my respect from them that way. I could play with them, so they couldn't take advantage of me."

Decades later, Genord said he regretted his decision to quit football as a freshman.

"I went through all the double sessions," he said. "I did all the hard work. All I had was the easy stuff left. I should have stayed."

Genord returned to the football field in 1960 as a sophomore and made up for lost time. He finished among the Catholic

League rushing and scoring leaders with a 13.3-yard average and 10 touchdowns.

There was at least one positive experience by a freshman slave. Dave Vitali showed up at St. Ambrose in 1958 as a runt-sized 5-2, 185 pounds and became the slave of Larry Bringard.

"Larry was a gentle giant and never a bully," Vitali said. "I always admired him."

As a trade off for polishing Bringard's cleats and carrying his equipment, Vitali became privy to the work ethic that would produce a prep All-America. He watched Bringard lift weight after weight off the field and block defender after defender on the field. Vitali wanted to become the next Bringard.

"My freshman year was uneventful," Vitali said. "I didn't get into games until they were out of reach. But after the season, I made up my mind that I must be a good football player because St. Ambrose recruited me to come there.

"So they asked me which number I wanted the next year. I was wearing No. 13. I told them I wanted Bringard's number (62). Boisture looked at Tobianski and said, 'What do you think, John? Can he handle it?' John said, 'Yeah, I think so.'

"So I started lifting weights. I started running and was determined to become a good football player. I made up my mind they would have to beat me to death to keep me from playing. I remember lining up against Mike Currie in fall practice and he wasn't making the block on me. So coaches started ragging on him, accusing him of dogging it. Mike said, 'Hey, coach, the kid's giving me a hard time. He's really working hard.' From that point on everyone looked at me differently."

Vitali went on to become a three-year starter and an all-state selection in 1961.

17

SEASON '59

Tom Boisture lined up a track team in his offensive backfield in 1959. Literally. Joe D'Angelo, Bill Fournier, and Larry Lantzy ran three legs of the St. Ambrose relay team that medaled in the East side track championships the previous spring. They were fast (D'Angelo), faster (Fournier), and fastest (Lantzy).

But Boisture decided to feature his smallest (5-8, 154 pounds) and slowest running back. D'Angelo would line up at halfback and be the primary ball carrier in the St. Ambrose Wing T. Vince Taormino would be the fullback, with Fournier and Lantzy providing a shuttle service at wingback. Boisture would use them as messengers to relay the plays to quarterback Manny Lamprides. So his two fastest players would rotate every other down.

Boisture wanted D'Angelo on the field every play. The St. Ambrose blocking front was never very big. At 5-11, 190 pounds, Fournier was bigger than a couple of the starting offensive linemen that season. D'Angelo offered the Cavaliers greater escapability than his two running mates. If the blocking broke down, D'Angelo had a better chance of turning a lemon of a play into lemonade than either Fournier or Lantzy.

"Joey had a quickness and the ability to cut," Boisture said. "The other two were faster but weren't as quick at the line of scrimmage. They could blow through, hit the seam and go. Billy ran all the reverses. He had that straight-line speed but he didn't have that wiggle. We utilized what we had — and we had speed at the wingback spot. Joey gave us the wiggle."

His teammates found Lantzy the most entertaining in practice and games because of his speed.

"He always ran the anchor on the relays," Pete Piazza said. "He had the jets. He flew. Give him an opening and he was gone."

But the Cavaliers found D'Angelo the most frustrating in practice because of his shiftiness.

"I remember trying to tackle him as a freshman," Ron Albers said. "It was impossible."

Boisture decided to change defensive schemes that season, tapping into the playbook of Chuck Fairbanks, an assistant coach at Arizona State at the time. Fairbanks would go on to greater heights as a head coach at the University of Oklahoma and the New England Patriots.

Fairbanks graduated from Michigan State and spent three years coaching at an Upper Peninsula high school before hooking on with Arizona State in 1958. Fairbanks still had strong ties with Duffy Daugherty and Michigan State, which had hired Tom's brother Dan as an assistant in 1959. Tom Boisture got to know Fairbanks in 1958 when he was recruiting Detroit.

Boisture was intrigued by the 5-2 slant defense favored by Fairbanks and spent many a night talking to him about it.

"Chuck was my edge," Boisture said. "They were always doing the latest thing when he was at Arizona State. He gave me all the information and insight on that defense."

Boisture liked the scheme because it gave linebacker Mike Currie the freedom to be a playmaker. Now a senior, Currie had filled out at 6-2, 190 pounds. Taormino, Lamprides, Skip Paoletti, Jerry Palazzola, and Gil Otts would join him as two-way starters that season. Jim Dinverno would step in at the other linebacker spot in the 5-2, filling the void created by the departures of Larry Bringard and Dave Brozo.

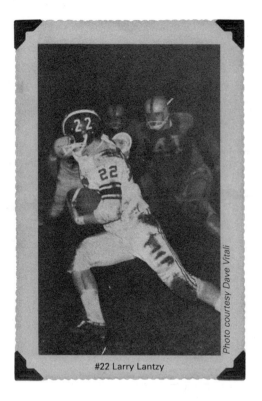

Photo courtesy Dave Vitali

#22 Larry Lantzy

"I may have given him the concepts of that defense," Fairbanks said, "but Tom still had to coach it and his players still had to execute it."

The Cavaliers proved quick learners. St. Ambrose scrimmaged Class A giants Grosse Pointe High and Southeastern before the season, and Boisture was starting to think his new defense could be as dominant as his offense.

"I remember toward the end of our scrimmage with Southeastern," Dinverno said. "We were pretty much wiping them up and on one play Tom told everyone on the defense not to go live except Mike and I. Everyone pretty much laid down — and they still couldn't gain any yards. I knew our defense was going to be pretty good. I knew our team was going to be pretty good."

Prep writer Joe Dowdall predicted in the *Detroit Free Press* St. Ambrose would reach its first Goodfellow Game. So Boisture wasn't the only football authority around town expecting a breakthrough year from the Cavaliers.

First up, St. Ladislaus.

"I was scared shitless that game," Boisture said. "They had one of the Pacioreks at quarterback."

That would be John, who would go on to play professional baseball for the Houston Colt .45s. His younger brother Tom also would come out of Hamtramck St. Lad's to play big-league baseball, spending 18 seasons with six teams.

"They were a much bigger team physically than us," said Paoletti of the Greyhounds.

But all the size and all the Pacioreks wouldn't matter. St. Ambrose won in a romp, 33-0, as Lantzy scored on runs of 64 and 21 yards and Lamprides threw TD passes to Fournier and Otts. There was one casualty against St. Ladislaus but it didn't occur until days later. Freshman quarterback Tom Beer broke his wrist in a junior varsity game against the Greyhounds that would sideline him until November.

The Cavaliers returned to Hamtramck for a second consecutive game at Keyworth Stadium against St. Florian. It was another romp, 46-12.

"Both St. Lad's and St. Florian's had really good athletes," Boisture said. "But they were baseball schools. We were a football school."

D'Angelo scored four touchdowns on runs of 63, 57, 51 and 1 yards. Backup quarterback Mike Tank threw TD passes of 65 yards to Lantzy and 54 yards to Fournier. But Vince Taormino suffered an ankle injury in the game, keeping him out of the offensive lineup for six weeks. He wasn't the only casualty.

"That was the first and last time my mom (Stella) ever saw me play," Dinverno said. "I got kicked in the mouth and got 10 stitches. I had two bars on my helmet. After that game, they gave me one of those bird cages. I was one of the first guys in the league to wear a bird cage. I was back at practice the following Monday."

The Cavaliers were 2-0 but untested. None of the Hamtramck schools had beaten St. Ambrose since Boisture became coach in 1956. But Pete Piazza learned there was no pleasing Boisture. The more the Cavaliers won, the harder they practiced and the more criticism they received from their head coach.

"The transition from grade school to high school was night and day," Piazza said. "The practices were long and hard and we could never do anything right. We'd play a game on a Friday night and Boisture would spend the weekend watching the films.

"We wouldn't have practice on Monday but we'd review the films. He could tell you what every player did wrong on every play. We'd watch one play 11 times and he'd point out every single mistake. There were times when D'Angelo would run, make a nice gain and Tom would say, 'Look at the way he's carrying that ball. You're so lucky you didn't fumble. You'd better get that ball tucked in or you'll be on the bench.' He was very much a disciplinarian."

The tougher games lie ahead and Boisture wanted his Cavaliers ready for them. St. Paul the next week was not one of them, but Boisture wanted to send a message to coach Ed Lauer for the throttling the Lakers gave the Cavaliers on the basketball court the previous season.

Mission accomplished — 46-12.

"They were a basketball school," Boisture said. "We were a football school."

D'Angelo turned in another four-touchdown game and had a fifth score nullified by penalty. Lantzy added a 34-yard touchdown run and Fournier an 11-yarder.

For the third consecutive week, the Cavaliers won wearing their maroon jerseys. St. Ambrose had four different color combinations for games — maroon jerseys and pants, white jerseys and pants, maroon tops and white bottoms or white tops and maroon bottoms.

It didn't matter to Boisture how the Cavaliers dressed as long as they were wearing the maroon jerseys. In 1957, when both St. Anthony and St. Ambrose both showed up with white jerseys for a game, Boisture quickly volunteered to wear the maroon tops.

"We hated the burgundy jerseys," Bill Lenhard said. "We always wanted to wear white on white. But Tom always wanted those burgundy jerseys because he wanted us to look small and the ball was tougher to find. When we came out on the field he'd tell us you looked bigger when you wear white on white. We hated them."

Boisture wanted to foist the "little" St. Ambrose image on his opponents. A little overconfidence on the other side never hurt. But more importantly, Boisture wanted Lamprides dealing from a maroon deck.

A leather football was easier to hide in the belly of a maroon jersey than a white one. Dark shirts enhanced the misdirection offense the Cavaliers were running.

"Lamprides was a magician with the ball," Paoletti said. "No one could handle it like he could. There was a lot of faking and movement in our backfield. It was like, 'Hey, here we come. We're going this way — no, we're going that way.'"

The opponents weren't the only folks on the field who couldn't keep their eye on the football in the Lamprides shell game.

"We had a touchdown called back that season because the officials lost track of the ball," Boisture said. "We had a lot of plays where they lost track of the ball so there'd be a quick whistle. Manny was very deceptive."

The Cavaliers were 3-0 and starting to feel good about themselves. Everyone seemed to be in a playful mood.

"I was sitting in the whirlpool one day and Skip comes in and tells John (Tobianski), 'This helmet doesn't fit too well,'" Lantzy said. "So John told him to leave it there and he'd fix it for him. So Skip set it on the table and John left it there for 10 minutes. Then John looks at me, winks and says, 'Hey, Paoletti, get in here.' He comes in and John says, 'Try it on now.' So Skip puts on the helmet and says, 'Ah, that's perfect, John.' Tobianski never touched the helmet. He looked at me and just shook his head."

The good times would continue with another trip to Keyworth to play the third and final Hamtramck school, St. Stanislaus. It was another romp, 40-0, as D'Angelo, Fournier and Lantzy combined for five touchdowns and Lamprides threw a 34-yard scoring pass to Currie.

"In some of those games — St. Florian, St. Ladislaus and St. Stanislaus — we could have scored more touchdowns than we did," D'Angelo said.

But the games would get tougher and more emotional from that point on for the 4-0 Cavaliers. The next opponent, Servite, was geographically the closest school to St. Ambrose in the Catholic East bracket, barely four miles apart. The players from the two schools went to the same pizza parlors and bowling alleys in the adjoining neighborhoods. Fisticuffs often broke out.

"We didn't like St. Anthony," Dinverno said, "but we hated Servite. The two schools were so close and they had pretty much an Italian team. We had a lot of Italians, too. Maybe it was the blood between us."

Servite also hadn't beaten St. Ambrose since Boisture's arrival. But this was the best team the Panthers had fielded in years. They would take a 4-0 record to Mack Park to play the Cavaliers in front of an expected crowd of almost 12,000.

But the St. Ambrose offense wouldn't be at full throttle. D'Angelo was nursing a swollen ankle and Lantzy a thigh bruise. Both would both suit up against Servite but would be there more in name than ability.

Photo courtesy Dave Vitali

St. Ambrose supporters

Still, St. Ambrose jumped out to a quick 14-0 lead on touchdown runs by Lamprides and Fournier. But Servite fought back to tie it. Mike Cure gave the Cavaliers a 21-14 lead on a 20-yard touchdown run in the fourth quarter, but Servite tied it a final time on a 1-yard run by Pat Chianetta with seven seconds remaining. Some pushing and shoving between the two teams ensued near the team busses after the 21-21 tie.

"That was like their Super Bowl," Lantzy said.

The Cavaliers were hot — first at Servite, then at themselves.

"The only way they scored was because of penalties," Fournier said. "We took a lot of unnecessary penalties that game. We had a roughing the kicker, a roughing this, a roughing that every time we stopped them. That's the only way they could score.

"It should have been 40-0. Talk about self-destruction. We did everything wrong and we still should have won. The game shouldn't have been close, yet we almost lost it."

Boisture was also in a funk. This wasn't supposed to happen.

"It was my fault," Boisture said. "It was my play-calling. I had enough running backs to beat those guys. I had enough of everything to beat those guys."

Captain Jim Cohanan stood up on the team bus after the game and told his teammates to settle down.

"We can still accomplish all that we set out to accomplish this season," he said. "It's still all there in front of us."

But the road suddenly seemed longer and now there was no margin for error.

"They caught us napping," Jack Cairo said. "They played beyond their potential and gave us a whale of a game. That might have been a wake-up call for us. I wouldn't call it a turning point for us — but it did make us leery that any team can beat any other. Maybe it told us we weren't as good as we thought we were. Maybe we needed to play better."

The task was becoming tougher by the week. Next up was St. Catherine, who was coming off a difficult 13-7 loss to St. Anthony. The 4-1 Warriors had been the preseason selection in some quarters to win the East and suited up one of the city's best linemen in Joe Henze.

The Cavaliers suffered a big blow in the second quarter when starting guard Bill Lenhard tore up a knee covering a kickoff on a blind-side chop block.

"I heard my knee snap and the pain was incredible," Lenhard said. "They didn't have an ambulance at the field and none of the stuff like they do today, so they had to go find a stretcher. They took me off the field into the locker room underneath Mack Park. I'm lying on the table still in incredible pain when Tom and the rest of the team came in at halftime. They're looking at me and I'm hyperventilating.

"Tom gave his whole halftime talk while I'm lying there. I can remember my best buddy Jack Cairo looking at me, his eyes this big, wondering, 'What is he doing?' As they are getting ready to go back on the field, Tom grabs my dad and says, 'Can you take him to the hospital?' So he gets the car, I hobble over and we go to Bon Secours. All I remember is waking up the next morning with a cast on my leg."

And his team 5-0-1. Perhaps stirred by the agonizing and emotional sight of Lenhard at halftime, the Cavaliers stormed to a 22-7 victory. Fournier scored on a 67-yard run and both D'Angelo and Taormino from shorter distances.

"They had some big boys, some mean guys," Fournier said. "They were a tough city team that played hard."

But all was not well in the Cavalier camp. Boisture held a healthy Dave Vitali out of the game.

"There was never an explanation," Vitali said. "As a 15-year-old, that was confusing."

When the bus returned to school, Vitali showered quickly and left in a huff, deciding to walk home the two miles in a driving rainstorm. He didn't get far.

"Jerry Palazzola and Dave Kulinski drove by with their dates," Vitali said. "They stopped the car and told me to get in. They drove me home and told me not to be mad, there must have been a legitimate reason I didn't play."

Vitali was never given that reason, and he continued to stew the next week.

"My dad could always tell how practice went by the way I came home walking between the houses," Vitali said. "If it was a good day I'd be singing or whistling. But on this day I didn't say anything. Then at dinner I started pissing and moaning about Boisture

Photo courtesy Dave Vitali

Dave Vitali

— 'That Boisture this...that Boisture that.' My dad was a Southern gentleman from Oklahoma. He told me, 'Boy, if it's too tough for you, quit.' I shut my mouth. I finished dinner, did my homework and never said another word about Tom Boisture to my dad."

Nor would Vitali need to. The next week, in the season finale against St. Anthony, he was in the starting lineup.

"They moved me to middle linebacker, which was Mike Currie's spot, and put him at defensive guard in a 6-1 (alignment)," Vitali said. "He was faster into the backfield. He could disrupt their play before it even started. Tom would always put his best man where he wanted him."

St. Anthony was already causing a disruption of its own. A few days before the game, several players from St. Anthony drove to St. Ambrose and circled the school in their convertibles, hooting and hollering about how they were going to take down the Cavaliers that week. The Teutons were 6-0 and coming off a 27-6 thrashing of Servite. No one had scored more than a single touchdown against St. Anthony all season.

"They were cocky and arrogant," Vitali said. "But Boisture always kept us under control. He'd tell us, 'If they talk to you, tell them just don't hurt us too bad because we've got another game to play next week.' They were yapping, 'You tied Servite and we beat them. Now we're going to whip you.' We never did a lot of talking."

It rained all week, leaving Mack Park a quagmire. A sloppy field figured to hurt a speed team like St. Ambrose. But it didn't. D'Angelo scored touchdowns on runs of 36 and 34 yards and Fournier added another score on a plunge in a 20-6 victory. Two other St. Ambrose touchdowns were nullified by penalty.

"We didn't play as well as we should have," Boisture said. "We should have beaten them a lot worse."

Conahan was right — everything the Cavaliers had hoped to achieve in 1959 was still in front of them. Their 6-0-1 record earned them the Catholic East title and a spot in the Soup Bowl against 5-0-2 Royal Oak Shrine.

But Shrine had a trump card for the game. The Knights were bringing their own Bishop to the Catholic League championship.

SOUP '59

Football put the St. Ambrose parish on the Catholic map in the 1950s. Shrine had already been on the map for decades.

The National Shrine of the Little Flower on Woodward Avenue in Royal Oak had been the home base of Father Charles Coughlin in the 1920s and 1930s. He was a political commentator who staged national radio broadcasts of his Sunday sermons. In the 1930s, Fr. Coughlin was Rush Limbaugh with a collar, criticizing President Franklin Delano Roosevelt and his New Deal.

Shrine was an emerging football power in the Catholic West in the late 1950s — and the Knights were emerging on the talented right arm of quarterback Ron Bishop.

Shrine finished 1-5 in 1956 and then went winless in 1957, failing to score more than six points in any game. But when Bishop hit the field in 1958, Shrine hit the win column. The Knights went 6-1 with that lone loss to St. Mary Redford. It kept Shrine out of the 1958 Soup Bowl.

But there was no stopping the Knights in 1959. Shrine shut out five of its seven opponents. The only blemishes on its record were a pair of ties with Holy Redeemer and St. Mary. Bishop was not only the best quarterback in the Catholic League, he was the best quarterback in all of Detroit. He earned all-city honors in 1959 and a scholarship to the University of Detroit.

Bishop completed 53 percent of his passes (56 of 105) for 1,071 yards and nine touchdowns. He rushed for two touchdowns and completed five more passes for extra-point conversions. His arm

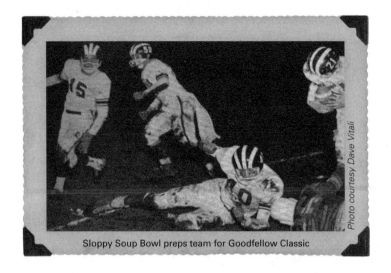

Sloppy Soup Bowl preps team for Goodfellow Classic

Photo courtesy Dave Vitali

generated a 46-0 victory over River Rouge Our Lady of Lourdes, a 38-0 romp over Detroit St. Theresa, and a 35-0 rout of Wyandotte Mount Carmel.

Prep writer Harvey Barcus of the *Detroit News* dubbed Bishop "the Johnny Unitas of prep high school circles." His primary target was John Seymour, the first in a long line of talented Seymours. Jim would also play for Shrine and become an All-America pass catcher at Notre Dame in the 1960s. Paul would play for Birmingham Brother Rice and become an All-America blocker at Michigan in the 1970s.

Shrine commanded the attention of St. Ambrose and every other Catholic in the Soup Bowl play-in game. All-boys school DeLaSalle captured the Central with a perfect record, allowing only 19 points in six games. But Bishop and the Knights vanquished the Pilots, 34-0, setting up the Soup Bowl showdown with St. Ambrose.

Tom Boisture clearly had a problem. His Cavaliers hadn't played a passing team all season — and didn't see one on the practice field, either. St. Ambrose went unbeaten itself because of the sleight of hand by quarterback Manny Lamprides, not his arm.

Boisture would have to be at his creative best to come up with a defensive scheme for Shrine. Bishop was a high-percentage passer well ahead of his time. Most high school teams had two ends that would catch passes. But Bishop had no reservations throwing to his running backs as well. There always seemed to be someone open — and Bishop had the patience and arm to get the football to him.

Boisture learned a little trick in his 44-6 Soup Bowl loss to DeLaSalle in 1956. Back then it was called a red dog. Today it's called a blitz. DeLaSalle discombobulated St. Ambrose quarterback John Jambor by sending linebackers after him that didn't usually rush the passer.

If Boisture dropped his linebackers into coverage, Bishop would have all day to throw and Shrine could play the Soup Bowl on his terms. By pressuring Bishop, St. Ambrose could force him to throw the ball before he was ready and take him out of his rhythm. DeLaSalle harassed Jambor into a three-interception night in that 1956 Soup Bowl.

So Boisture devised a scheme that would sink five players into pass coverage. He assigned linebacker Mike Currie, his best defender, to shadow whichever Knight came circling out of the backfield. Then he incorporated Jim Dinverno, the other linebacker in the 5-2 scheme, into the pass rush.

Boisture also moved Lamprides back to a deep safety position. If anyone on St. Ambrose could figure out where Bishop was going to throw the football, Boisture guessed it would be his own quarterback. Lamprides would be the last line of defense against Shrine and could get a jump on any ball Bishop did throw. Every play would unfold in front of him. In essence, Boisture had devised a prevent defense years ahead of its time.

Boisture believed he had an offense that could score on Shrine. Why not? The Cavaliers had averaged 33 points per game themselves that season, and Joe D'Angelo was every bit the running threat that Bishop was as a passer. Boisture just wasn't sure if his Cavaliers could generate enough points to outscore Shrine.

Fate seemed to be conspiring against the Cavaliers that second weekend of November. The rains continued in Detroit, producing another soggy field not conducive to the St. Ambrose speed. And the Detroit Public School League had staged its championship game the night before the Soup Bowl at the very same University of Detroit stadium. Cooley carved up Eastern, 26-13, and the two teams carved up the field. Freezing temperatures on the eve of the Soup Bowl produced yet another quagmire for the Cavaliers.

"It was muddy and sloppy," wingback Larry Lantzy said. "You'd run and feel these deep ridges in the field. You'd step on some ice and your foot would sink into six inches of water. The field was a mess."

St. Ambrose also was assigned to wear its dreaded white jerseys for the game. So there would be no hide-and-seek of the football for Shrine. Every fake by Lamprides would be fully visible against a white backdrop.

St. Ambrose trainer John Tobianski dug into his equipment trunk to find some edges for his team on this bitter cold and sloppy night.

"John had these brown work gloves and he gave them to the offensive linemen to wear," Dave Vitali said. "He also got goggles for D'Angelo, Cairo, (Tom) Milton and (Jim) McKee. They were prescription goggles. The only other teams wearing them at the time were in the colleges and pros."

Ron Bishop was great that night — but D'Angelo was greater. D'Angelo burst 56 yards for a touchdown in the first quarter and 73 yards for another score in the second. Conversion runs by Lantzy and Currie gave the Cavaliers a stunning 14-0 halftime lead.

The defense was holding Bishop and the explosive Knights — but for how long? Dinverno continued crashing the backfield.

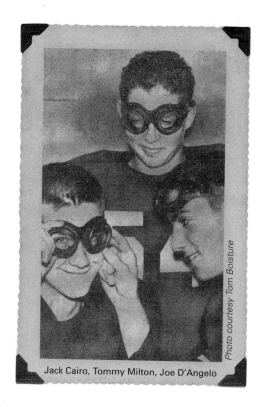

Jack Cairo, Tommy Milton, Joe D'Angelo

Photo courtesy Tom Boisture

"I was trying to get to Bishop the whole game," he said. "I kept trying to jump over their guy and he kept flipping me. I'm surprised I didn't lose any legs that night."

Currie cancelled out the swing passes to the backs, forcing Bishop to throw the ball down the field to the ends. Lamprides would be waiting there to break up his heaves.

The Cavaliers had an anxious moment in the third quarter. They sat on 14 points at half and were done scoring for the night. Mike Cure would have to carry St. Ambrose the rest of the way with his punting. The Cavaliers had a freshman, Mike Goff, snapping the ball.

"Mike was on the 10-yard line," Goff recalled, "and I snapped it over his head. It was the only time I ever snapped one over anyone's head in my life. He ran back into the end zone, scooped it up and brought it back out to the 2. We wound up holding them."

But the Cavaliers couldn't hold Shrine out of the end zone all night. Bishop hit Seymour with a 29-yard touchdown pass in the fourth quarter to cut the deficit to 14-6. But Bishop slipped on the messy field and his conversion run failed.

St. Ambrose held on for a 14-6 victory. D'Angelo was spectacular, motoring through the slop as if he was the only guy playing on a dry field. He rushed 17 times for 214 yards, a staggering 12.6-yard average. Fournier, Lantzy and the rest of the St. Ambrose backfield chipped in another 115 yards. In an interesting twist, Boisture dabbled with All-Catholic end Mike Currie, moving him inside to guard for a handful of plays.

Bishop wasn't his usual accurate self against the Cavaliers, completing only 19 of his 38 throws. But the weather conditions contributed to several other drops, including a sure touchdown by Seymour at the St. Ambrose 3 in the second quarter. In a valiant effort, Bishop riddled a St. Ambrose defense stacked against him for 275 yards. But he got no help from his running game. Shrine rushed for only 21 yards.

"It was a great job by our defense," Boisture said. "The kid could really throw the ball. Blitzing wasn't popular then, but I probably should have sent Currie a few more times. We knew we had to stop the pass."

Dan Boisture won four Catholic League titles at Redford St. Mary. His little brother Tom finally won his first. But Dan had a victory in a Goodfellow Game in his back pocket. Tom did not. And it wasn't likely he'd get his first in 1959 against the mighty Cooley Cardinals.

COOLEY

Tom Boisture didn't need to watch any game film to see how talented the Public School League champions were. All he had to do was phone his brother Dan, who had become an assistant coach at Michigan State in 1959.

"He was recruiting half their team," Boisture said.

And for good reason. The Cooley Cardinals were loaded. Their center Gus Kasapis was a behemoth, listed in the program as 6-3, 268 pounds. He doubled as the nose guard on defense and was an all-state selection. Kasapis was the PSL's Defensive Player of the Year and would receive a scholarship to Iowa.

Kasapis was joined on the all-city team by running back Bill Kelley, who averaged 8.2 yards per carry and scored 10 touchdowns. He also passed for five touchdowns on options and intercepted four passes as a defensive back. Cooley had a third member of the All-PSL team in guard Larry Scroby. Also on the Cardinals was end Doug Roberts, who would become an All-America hockey player at Michigan State and go on to play in the NHL.

Individually, the Cardinals were good. Collectively, they were even better. Arguably, the best. The Associated Press ranked Cooley No. 1 in Class A, the state's big-school classification. The Cardinals stormed to the top spot with eight consecutive victories, most by lopsided scores.

After a 12-7 nail-biter in the season opener against Redford and its own all-state running back Dave Vollmer, Cooley blew through McKenzie (39-6), Murray Wright (47-0), Cody (40-7),

Western (34-13), Southwestern (27-0), and Northwestern (27-7) to win the West and claim a slot in the PSL title game.

But PSL East champion Eastern was a talented team in its own right with a 6-0-1 record. Tackle Louis Proctor was an all-city selection and running back Bob Grier joined him on the All-PSL team. Eastern also had a gifted sophomore lineman named Bill Yearby, who would go on to become an All-America at the University of Michigan and a first-round draft pick of the New York Jets. Grier himself would fashion an NFL career, spending more than a quarter of a century in coaching and personnel with the New England Patriots and Houston Texans.

"Other than Redford in our first game of the year, everything else was pretty easy until we got to Eastern," Cooley running back Ross MacDonald said.

Eastern negotiated the mud at the University of Detroit stadium better than Cooley in the first half of the PSL title game, building a 13-7 lead.

"We couldn't move the ball," said Cooley coach Roger Parmentier. "They should have beaten us. But there are three phases of football — offense, defense, and special teams. We beat them by returning punts, kickoffs, and interceptions for touchdowns."

The Cardinals prevailed, 26-13, and figured they had already beaten the toughest foe they would face all year. St. Ambrose? The Catholic school wasn't even ranked in Class C heading into the Goodfellow Game. Cooley was considered the best team in the entire state regardless of class.

"Often times the newspapers didn't pay that much attention to a school like St. Ambrose like they would a Cooley or Denby because we were always ranked in the Top 10," Parmentier said. "But those are mythical rankings. That's supposed to give you prestige. Come that game you're undefeated, you're No. 1 in the state, and you've got all those big guys playing against little St. Ambrose."

Photo courtesy Tom Boisture, by Detroit Times

Boisture vs. Parmentier

Tom Boisture and Cooley Coach Roger Parmentier face off before the Goodfellow Game in an interview by R. P. Jones on WQTE radio.

The three Detroit newspapers — the *Free Press, News,* and *Times* — documented the differences between the two teams and schools in the week leading up to the game.

Cooley was an educational giant with an enrollment of 3,474. St. Ambrose's enrollment was a modest 396 students, including only 140 boys. Cooley's offensive and defensive lines averaged 216 pounds. The St. Ambrose line averaged 184. Cooley had a bigger running back (210-pound fullback Art Hanoian) than any St. Ambrose blocker.

Then there was the Gus Kasapis problem facing the Cavaliers. He was a one-man wrecking crew in the middle of the Cooley defense, blocking four punts and forcing three fumbles returned for touchdowns in 1959. Kasapis would have almost a 100-pound weight advantage on St. Ambrose center Skip Paoletti.

"They took a picture of my line and put it in the newspaper," Parmentier said. "Back then we were bigger than the Detroit Lions. They were mooses. Kasapis was close to 300. He was huge."

How would — could — the Cavaliers block the biggest and best lineman in the city? If St. Ambrose needed to invest three lineman in containing Kasapis, how would its remaining seven block Cooley's 10?

This game screamed mismatch. But Parmentier knew better.

Parmentier was familiar with the East side of town. He lived in East Detroit and attended St. Veronica. At one point he was a part-time police officer in Grosse Pointe Park, and his aunt and uncle owned a chicken store a block away from St. Ambrose.

"I knew about St. Ambrose from the time I was a little guy," Parmentier said. "They were never a football power until they started hiring good coaches. They were a program destined to become better. Good coaches attract good athletes."

Boisture was a good coach. Parmentier discovered that in the fall. The public schools played their games at 3:30 on Friday afternoons. That gave Parmentier the freedom to scout the Catholic League games on Friday and Saturday nights and Sunday afternoons.

"I went and watched everybody," Parmentier said. "There was no question in my mind we'd be playing St. Ambrose. I saw a well-coached football team that had great athletes and a lot of unity. They had some close games that year but they were a bunch of scrappers who believed in their coach."

The Cooley players were reading one story line in the newspapers but hearing quite a different story line from their coach. The Cardinals attended the Soup Bowl as a team and watched St. Ambrose hold on for dear life against a one-dimensional Shrine team.

"My guys didn't believe me," Parmentier said. "They couldn't believe St. Ambrose was that good. Our players told me, 'Those guys are like little flies. They're small and they're not that fast.' I'd say, 'Hey, they're football players. Trust me. They are good athletes that are well-coached. They'll give us a bunch of trouble.'"

Parmentier knew Boisture would have something up his sleeve for the Goodfellow Game. He just didn't know what.

PRAYER

For the first time in St. Ambrose history, the Cavaliers would have a decided advantage over a football opponent — prayer.

Finally, St. Ambrose would be playing a public school. The Cavaliers could pray for victory against Cooley with the faith, knowledge, and confidence their prayers would be answered. When two Catholic schools play, the prayers tended to cancel each other out. But God wouldn't have to choose sides in the Goodfellow Game.

"That was all part of the Catholic school shtick," Larry Lantzy said. "As you get older, you realize the other guys were praying, too. Why didn't Notre Dame win every game?"

But no one prayed like St. Ambrose.

"We were a holy team," Marshall Houle mused.

The Cavaliers spent as much time at church as they did on the practice field. Every day before class, the entire school — all 12 grades — would file into St. Ambrose's gothic cathedral for 8 o'clock mass. The football team also went to Mass *en masse* on Saturday and on Sunday mornings.

"Every morning," cackled Mike Van Goethem decades later. "I shouldn't have to go to Mass for another 40 years because I've done my time."

The last thing the Cavaliers did before loading the bus at school for a game was stop by church for a prayer. They'd troop into the church in full uniform except for the cleats. They'd walk the granite floor in their stocking feet and kneel at the altar rail that stretched

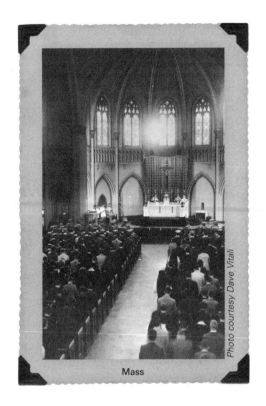

Photo courtesy Dave Vitali

Mass

across the front of the church. Then the first thing the Cavaliers did upon their return from games was to revisit the church, kneeling in the dark at the front steps to offer up a prayer of thanks.

"We led the league in prayer," Tom Beer said.

Actually, stopping off at church was the third thing the Cavaliers would do upon their return.

The maroon and white school bus — another gift of Dad's Club dollars — would come chugging down Alter Road after games. The bus was usually awash with noise and exuberance following another St. Ambrose victory. They were becoming quite commonplace under Tom Boisture.

At the intersection of Alter and St. Paul, a block away from the school, the football team would burst out singing the school fight song. Loudly. Proudly.

John Tobianski, the bus driver, would make that left turn onto Hampton and pull up in front of the school, where the Cavaliers would receive a thunderous and boisterous welcome from what seemed to be the entire student body plus parents and parishioners.

"You've got to understand that school meant everything to that little neighborhood," Dave Brozo said.

The players, still in full uniform, would exit the bus and walk across Hampton to the side door of the convent, where they would be greeted, congratulated and hugged by the nuns.

"They'd beat us up in school," Pete Genord said, "but they always seemed happy to see us after a football game."

Then the players would troop that half block up Hampton for the final prayer of the night — and the week — at the church steps.

All sounds hokey, doesn't it?

"No siree," Boisture said. "Nothing corny about the church steps. [John] Jambor and that bunch weren't overly religious, but that meant something to them. I was surprised. They were doing it before I arrived. That was all handled by the team. They felt comfortable doing it. It was almost like a superstition."

The praying didn't end at the church. Every fall the nuns would cut little brown footballs out of construction paper and write the name and jersey number of a Cavalier on each. Every classroom would have a football tacked to its bulletin board, and each day during homeroom the class would pray for the health and safety of that player.

That was the first of many prayers in class that day. Sister Mary Ellen Plummer was another parish lifer who attended St. Ambrose. She had a brother who played on the school's 1961 championship team. The nuns took winning seriously.

"On the Friday of a game we prayed extra hard not only for a victory but that no one would be seriously hurt," she said. "Oh how we prayed. Every hour, on the hour, we faced the Infant of Prague statue in the classroom and prayed, 'Oh God, you taught us: ask and you shall receive, seek and you shall find, knock and it shall be opened for you...we knock, we seek, we ask that our prayer be granted.'

"Then, in the silence that followed, everyone — the sisters, lay teachers, students — squeezed out the biggest 'Puh-leeeeze' that the Almighty had ever heard. Or at least since the last hour. It was all pretty intense."

Even when the games were being played and everyone was focused on the action on the field, there were prayers being said on behalf of the Cavaliers. That's because the Dominican order did not allow the nuns to attend the games. So they spent the evening in the convent, many of them saying the rosary.

"The nuns embraced the football program," Ray Malcoun said. "I don't know that you ever got any special breaks being a football player, but you sure felt their support."

The nuns may have fired a few blackboard erasers at football players in the classroom and rapped a few knuckles with pointers and blackboard compasses. That was their job — to teach. But their pride and passion was the football team.

"They were tough ladies," Mike Van Goethem said. "They lived there and the school was their life. It was very important to them that you learned something. They'd never admit it, but they used to be almost as excited about the football team as we were."

But it would take more than a convent full of nuns in hourly prayer for St. Ambrose to defeat Cooley.

GAME PLAN

Joe D'Angelo was the king of St. Ambrose. He was the most valuable player on the best Catholic team in the city.

D'Angelo rushed the ball 70 times through the Soup Bowl for 1,120 yards, an amazing average of 16 yards per carry. He scored 15 touchdowns, including nine on sprints of 30 yards or more. As small as he (5-8, 154) and his school was, D'Angelo was still the Big Man on Campus at St. Ambrose.

"You were treated like a star," D'Angelo said. "You tried to be humble but everyone treated you like a hero. But Boisture had a way of keeping things in perspective."

The Cavaliers had one week to prepare for the Goodfellow Game. On Monday of that week, Mike Currie and D'Angelo drove downtown to the *Detroit News* to participate in a photo shoot for the newspaper's all-city football team. They returned to school barely in time for practice.

"I was probably strutting around a little bit," D'Angelo conceded. "So Tom made me go down and practice with the freshmen that day just to show me, 'Hey, Joe, don't start thinking you're that good.' At the time it was humiliating. But looking back now, I can see why he did that."

Teams win, not players. If the Cavaliers were to upset Cooley in the city championship game, it would take a team effort. No one player was bigger than the team.

And that's what the Cavaliers appreciated about their coach.

"Tom was very consistent," Pete Piazza said. "You could have been the superstar or the 45th guy on the bench and you were treated the same way. He'd call you out. Nobody got a pass. D'Angelo was sweating up and down doing sprints just like the rest of us that week. Nobody got excused from anything.

"I learned at a very young age when someone treats everyone consistently, it's an easier pill to swallow."

D'Angelo working at the other end of the field with freshmen Piazza, Ron Albers, Tom Beer, and Mike Goff wasn't the only surprise awaiting the Cavaliers upon their return to practice. There was a bigger surprise awaiting the offensive linemen. A much bigger surprise.

Joe Henze was in uniform ready to practice with the Cavaliers. The same Joe Henze who was an all-state defensive tackle at St. Catherine. The same Joe Henze who gave St. Ambrose blockers fits just three weeks earlier at Mack Park.

"We didn't know he was coming over until he got there," D'Angelo said.

Boisture and St. Catherine coach Mike Rhodes were close friends. They talked all the time. That Sunday Boisture and Rhodes discussed the monumental problem facing St. Ambrose in the Goodfellow Game — Cooley's 268-pound nose tackle Gus Kasapis. His kids had never played against a guy that size.

Rhodes offered to send over his own 230-pound nose guard Henze to give the undersized St. Ambrose blockers a preview in practice of what was to come.

"Our kids were friends with the St. Catherine kids," Boisture said. "They wanted to help us beat Cooley and win the championship."

But first, Henze would beat up on interior linemen Skip Paoletti, Ray DeVriendt, and Ray Federspiel in practice. Not a one weighed 190.

"Boisture always had us prepared," D'Angelo said. "Knowing we were going against Kasapis, he brought over the toughest kid from St. Catherine with one responsibility — beat up our centers. He came over and basically kicked our butt."

The middle of the St. Ambrose line had been unsettled ever since the St. Catherine game when Lenhard tore up a knee. Jerry Palazzola was set at right guard but DeVriendt, Federspiel, and Paoletti rotated through the other two spots. Federspiel had been the primary starter at center all season. Paoletti started at center in the Soup Bowl, but DeVriendt would replace him in the lineup against Cooley.

"I had the feeling that was going to happen after practicing with (Henze)," said Federspiel, who missed Henze and the St. Catherine game the first go-round with the flu. "He kicked the shit out of me. Kasapis was as good or better than this guy. I'm certain that's what Boisture was looking at."

Offensive line coach Bud Kurvink wasn't happy with what he was seeing, either. If they couldn't neutralize Henze, how were the Cavaliers going to neutralize a player 40 pounds heavier and every bit as fast? Jim Conahan was St. Ambrose's best linemen. He could give Kasapis a tussle. But he was a long way off at right tackle.

"Bud said we needed someone at guard, no matter where Conahan is," Boisture recalled. "Jim wasn't going to get the chance to block Kasapis unless he blocked down. We needed someone to block head up on Kasapis."

In 1968, Mayo Smith made a daring switch in the World Series as manager of the Detroit Tigers. He moved his Gold Glove center fielder Mickey Stanley to shortstop to get Al Kaline into the lineup against the St. Louis Cardinals. Kaline hit .379, Stanley committed only two errors, and the Tigers won the World Series.

Boisture made a bold move of his own. He took his all-state end Mike Currie and moved him to guard for the Goodfellow Game. D'Angelo may have been St. Ambrose's most valuable player in 1959 — but Currie was its best player.

"Mike was our best blocker," Boisture said. "He also was our best athlete. He was strong, tough. No question he was our fastest lineman. He was probably the fastest guard in the state. In the Wing T we were pulling our guards every other play. We needed someone in there to handle their best player and also someone to get out in front of our backs."

Currie had a week to learn the entire playbook at guard. Boisture left it intact except for one addition, which would feature Currie's speed and athleticism. Play "132" was a handoff to D'Angelo off right tackle. The new play was called "132 Special." It was the same play except for a "special" twist — Currie pulling and leading D'Angelo through the hole.

But Boisture wasn't done yet strapping the hopes of a team, school and parish onto the broad shoulders of Currie.

Blocking Kasapis might be the least of St. Ambrose's worries. If the Cavaliers couldn't find a way to stand up to Cooley's "Mooses" and slow down the Cardinals on offense, they wouldn't have to worry about blocking Kasapis. St. Ambrose would never have the football. The Cardinals could grind down the tiny Cavaliers as they had Cody and Murray Wright.

So Boisture started the week from scratch on defense.

"What did we have to lose?" Boisture said. "They outmanned us. I had some midgets. Dave Kulinski was my heaviest guy and he couldn't play a full game. We could slant them, but we knew we couldn't do that all night because if one guy misses a tackle, it's a touchdown.

"Miles [Currie] was in charge of our defense. So he says to me, 'Let's put in the defense that gave us the hardest time this season.'"

That meant another phone call to Mike Rhodes. Tell me more about your 7-1 defensive scheme, Boisture said.

"It was a bitch," Boisture said. "We couldn't stop Henze. He'd kill us. Mike [Rhodes] would line up his nose tackle on the center, then back him off. It was something nobody else was doing and it was a

Photo courtesy Tom Boisture

Mike Currie

helluva defense. But we figured it out. We had their guys chasing the ball in the wrong direction because of all the deception.

"The scheme was designed to protect Henze. We had to find a way to protect Mike Currie."

On Monday, Boisture implemented his own 7-1 defensive front with Currie the roving middle linebacker.

"I had to put him in a position where he could make plays," Boisture said. "So we'd have seven guys occupying people at the line of scrimmage and let Mike chase the ball. This defense would allow him to run sideline to sideline. He made the big plays for us all year and we wanted to give him the chance to make them in the Goodfellow Game."

So Boisture was staking his upset hopes on the versatility of Mike Currie and the element of surprise.

"I knew we could score on them because of Manny and the offense," Boisture said. "How many times, I didn't know. And I figured we could confuse them on defense. They wouldn't be able to figure it out. You're dealing with high-school kids."

In the biggest game of his coaching life, Boisture would re-work his approach on both sides of the ball. But he had less than a week to implement the changes and convince the Cavaliers they could topple the best team in the state. The Detroit newspapers were touting Cooley as a 14-point favorite.

"I can remember during the season Tom saying, 'All I want to do is get to the Goodfellow Game,'" Larry Lantzy said. "But that week he told us, 'Getting there ain't good enough. We're going to win the Goodfellow Game.'"

BRIGGS

The Old Newsboys Goodfellow Fund was established in 1914 with the motto, "No kiddie without a Christmas."

Each year the Old Newsboys would raise money for Christmas gift boxes of books, clothes, toys, and candy given to needy children in the Detroit area.

The second Monday in December was always a big day for the Old Newsboys. In a joint venture with the local newspapers, the "Goodfellows" would stand on street corners that day and peddle papers with all proceeds going to their fund.

The Goodfellow Game was the other big day for the Old Newsboys. The game pitting the parochial and public school champions was established in 1938. The Old Newsboys secured Briggs Stadium, the cavernous home of the NFL's Detroit Lions on Michigan Avenue, as the site.

The public schools built an 11-8-2 lead in the series through 1958 with only two parochial schools proving competitive on a regular basis, Catholic Central and Redford St. Mary. They combined for 13 of the Catholic League appearances and six of the victories.

The bigger the schools, the bigger the turnout. Denby and Redford St. Mary drew a record crowd of 39,004 in 1948. When Redford High squared off against Redford St. Mary in 1958, all of Redford seemed to pass through the turnstiles that night, producing a crowd of 38,896.

The Old Newsboys weren't sure what to expect for the 1959 game. Cooley had a strong following befitting the size of the school, twice drawing crowds in excess of 30,000 for Goodfellow appearances. But St. Ambrose was a tiny Class C school with a small enrollment, making its Briggs Stadium debut. Tickets ranged from $1 to $4 and, weather permitting, the Old Newsboys were hoping to again attract a crowd in the 30,000s.

Prep writer Hal Schram of the *Detroit Free Press* did not expect much of a contest, writing throughout the week about the advantage Cooley had in size. He labeled the game a battle between David and Goliath.

But on the eve of the Goodfellow Game, Tom Boisture seemed more concerned with the size of the stadium than the size of the Cardinals.

Briggs Stadium was a giant step up from Mack Park both in structure and aura. The Detroit Tigers played baseball there in the summer. The Detroit Lions played football there in the fall. Filled to capacity, the triple-deck stadium could hold in excess of 56,000.

The previous Sunday, the Lions thumped the Los Angeles Rams, 23-17, before a crowd of 52,247 at Briggs Stadium. The Cavaliers would regularly draw 9,000 to Mack Park, which only had stands along the two sidelines. The biggest crowd the Cavaliers had ever entertained was 15,247 the previous week in the Soup Bowl at the University of Detroit.

The crowd for the Goodfellow Game would be double that, and the enclosed nature of Briggs Stadium would amplify the sound. Boisture was concerned the stage might be too big for his Cavaliers.

"Don't look up," Boisture cautioned his team on the Thursday before the game. "The field is 100 yards long, just like Mack Park. Just play the game."

Boisture had another paranoia that week. He was concerned Cooley might spy on his practices at Defer. St. Ambrose practiced on a public playground that was wide open on three sides. The homes on Balfour protected the fourth side of the field East of Defer. There were no tarps on the fences that became so common-place at football practice fields by the 1990s.

Anyone could stroll up to the fence or sit on the playground swingset and watch…and what anyone saw might surprise them. There were no goalposts on the field. There were no chalk designations of yard lines or sidelines. The Cavaliers stored a few blocking dummies in a small shed near the school. The Catholic League champions certainly were a Spartan bunch.

"It really wasn't much of a field," Ray Malcoun said. "I don't think it was long enough to put 100 yards in any direction. And by the end of the year it was all dust."

But Boisture kept his concerns to himself. He tried to stick as closely to his team's normal routine as possible that week. He wanted to convey the impression that Cooley was just another game.

On game day, the team walked up to Captain Shumway's restaurant on Jefferson after school for its weekly pre-game meal. The Dad's Club picked up the tab. For Saturday games, the Cavaliers dined on steak and baked potatoes. But the Goodfellow Game fell on a Friday night, and Catholics didn't eat meat on Fridays. So the Cavaliers ate fish.

Then the players walked back to the school. Even though it was several hours before the game, they donned their football pants and sweat socks. John Tobianski was taping all the ankles, his weekly routine. The players could look up from the training tables and see Tobianski's favorite sign on the wall: We Supply Everything But Guts.

Then the Cavaliers marched up the few stairs out of the locker room into the darkened hallway in the basement of the school. There they sat on the stone floor. There was silence for the next hour.

"You'd either pray or think," Larry Lantzy said. "It was all football. There was no music or joking around."

Briggs Stadium

Photo courtesy stadiumsofnfl.com

Then the Cavaliers finished suiting up and, after a quick stop at the church for a final prayer, boarded a bus for the drive downtown. The school's maroon-and-white bus remained in Tobianski's backyard that night. The Dad's Club rented a Greyhound to transport the players to the biggest game of their lives. More silence.

The Cavaliers picked up a police escort along the way and pulled into the stadium parking lot off Trumbull. The huge grids of blazing lights atop the third deck of the stadium reminded the Cavaliers that they were no longer Mack Park's team.

A small handful of Ambrosians had been involved in games at Briggs Stadium in the past — but none of this magnitude.

Boisture, of course, had coached Austin in the Catholic League championship baseball game there in 1955. In 1956, Tom Beer and his Cannon Tars played a brief Little League football game at halftime of an NFL game between the Lions and New York Giants. And just the previous spring, Mike Goff played in the CYO championship baseball game for St. Veronica there against Ss. Peter & Paul. Like Boisture, he lost.

"They beat us in extra innings in front of a standing-room-only crowd of about 120," Goff mused.

There would be considerably more spectators at Briggs Stadium this night. The Cavaliers were designated as the road team, so they were assigned the locker room used by visiting NFL teams. It would be the same locker room where Mike Currie's brother Dan and the Green Bay Packers would suit up to play the Lions in the traditional Thanksgiving Day game the following week.

"I remember walking in that locker room and being in awe, knowing we were playing where the Lions play," Joe D'Angelo said.

Then came the pre-game warm-ups. The freshmen were the first to hit the field. The starters would come out a short time later.

"Coming out of the tunnel, through the dugout onto the field was interesting," Ron Albers said. "We were just high school kids and our helmets would hit the top of the tunnel. I was thinking, 'How the hell are these pros coming through here?'"

Mike Van Goethem was among the first on the field. Barring absolute disaster, he would not play. He barely played all season. Another night on the bench might be advisable for him on this night.

"Seeing all that green grass and all those people, you wondered, 'What the hell are we doing here?'" Van Goethem said. "It was scary."

Against Boisture's caution, Lantzy did look up when he motored onto the field for pre-game warmups.

"We weren't used to playing in a bowl where the stands were all around you," Lantzy said. "It was terribly exciting. The field was well-manicured. You just wanted to pinch yourself and say, 'Is this really happening to me?' We were all sky high that night."

The sight of the Cooley Cardinals trotting out of their dugout onto the field jarred the Cavaliers back to reality. Not only were the Cardinals bigger in size, they were greater in number. Cooley was suiting up 44 players that night, St. Ambrose 41. The Cavaliers read all week how big the Cardinals were. Now they got to see that size up close.

Van Goethem was 14 years old and barely 140 pounds. He didn't fear for his own safety — he feared for the safety of the guy ahead of him on the depth chart, D'Angelo.

"He was as small as I was," Van Goethem said. "I thought, 'He's going to get killed out there. They're going to eat him up.'"

The Cavaliers returned to their locker room as bigger underdogs than they were an hour earlier. Boisture tried to put the challenge in perspective in his final words to the team.

"Out of all the teams we've played against, we earned this," Boisture told the Cavaliers. "We practiced hardest, played the hardest. Think back to how many times you've run around that football field. The conditioning, the wind sprints. It would be a darn shame to come this far and have this team knock us off."

Boisture didn't puff his team up with false bravado.

"Everyone says we're going to lose," he said, "but we'll make it interesting."

Jack Cairo found his choice of words interesting.

"He didn't say if we were going to win or lose," Cairo recalled.

Boisture recruited Salesian coach Frank Buford and Hamtramck coach Art May to work the game in the press box for him, giving St. Ambrose extra sets of eyes in the sky. Buford also worked the press box in the previous Goodfellow Game as an assistant at Redford St. Mary for Tom's brother Dan.

"Art and Frank probably knew our offense better than I did," Boisture said. "I stole from them all the time. I give to them, they'd give to me."

Boisture invited one final person to join the St. Ambrose traveling party — Fr. George Rozman, who was now at a parish in Monroe.

"Father Van Antwerp wanted a football program," Boisture said. "But it was Father Rozman who built the program. He deserved to be there. It was as much his program as any of us."

GOODFELLOW 1

A crowd of 38,896 — the third largest in Goodfellow history — greeted the two teams upon their return to the field. There also was a citywide radio audience with Van Patrick, the voice of the Detroit Lions, providing the play-by-play. Welcome to the big time, St. Ambrose.

Next came the price for that sudden fame — a game with the No. 1 team in the state of Michigan. Once again, the Cavaliers were forced to wear their white jerseys.

Cooley won the coin toss and elected to receive. Ted Bytnar returned Dave Kulinski's short kickoff 25 yards to the 40. Two plays later, Bill Kelley circled right end for 24 yards to the St. Ambrose 38. Starting defensive tackle Dave Vitali was sprawled on the field. He entered the game nursing a charley horse and was chopped down at the thigh by a body block at the whistle.

"My game was over," Vitali said. "I couldn't walk for two months after that. I watched the rest of that game from the bench."

A thin team was becoming even thinner. Dave Kulinski, who "couldn't play a full game," according to Boisture, would now have to play a full game in Vitali's absence. The night appeared to be unraveling quickly on the Cavaliers.

But Manny Lamprides wasn't fazed. Nothing fazed him. He was the James Dean of St. Ambrose. With his flattop haircut, Lamprides was cool when cool was still in its infancy in this country.

"He was one of the only guys I knew who'd smoke in front of the coaches," Ron Albers said.

"He figured out early he was the only quarterback Boisture had," Mike Van Goethem said. "What the hell could they do to him?"

Lamprides had confidence in his abilities. All of the Cavaliers did. He was the firing pin of the offense.

"When we first got there as freshmen, we're sitting in the hall watching the varsity on offense," Mike Goff said. "Manny got behind center and said, 'Ready...set...hut...hut...' When they moved, we'd never seen anything that fast in our life. We almost laughed. It was like being at a carnival."

The Cavaliers looked for Joe D'Angelo to deliver the big plays on offense and Mike Currie to deliver the big plays on defense. But they looked for Lamprides to provide the swagger — and he gave them that swagger in the early going against Cooley.

On Cooley's fourth play of the game, Kelley again attempted to sweep right end. But Lamprides came charging up from his safety spot for a defensive trifecta — a tackle, forced fumble and fumble recovery. First down, St. Ambrose at its own 30. The Cavaliers dodged their first bullet.

Three plays into St. Ambrose's first possession, Lamprides ran a bootleg pass. Throwing the ball was not his strength. He hadn't tossed a touchdown pass in his last four games and didn't even complete a pass in seven tries against Shrine in the Soup Bowl. But on this play he found Mike Currie 33 yards down the field for a first down at the Cooley 30.

Forget the fact Lamprides threw an interception to Cooley captain Ross MacDonald three plays later on a jump pass to Currie. The early attempts served a purpose — they forced the Cardinals to acknowledge the pass, backing some of that Cooley size away from the line of scrimmage. That would give the St. Ambrose running backs a smidgen of daylight.

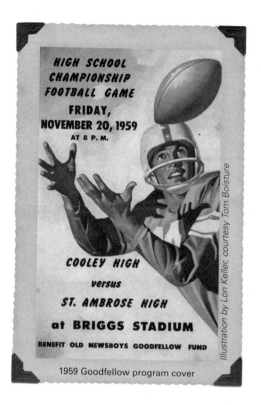

HIGH SCHOOL CHAMPIONSHIP FOOTBALL GAME
FRIDAY, NOVEMBER 20, 1959
AT 8 P. M.

COOLEY HIGH

versus

ST. AMBROSE HIGH

at BRIGGS STADIUM

BENEFIT OLD NEWSBOYS GOODFELLOW FUND

Illustration by Lon Keller, courtesy Tom Boisture

1959 Goodfellow program cover

Four plays later, Currie met Cooley halfback Ross MacDonald square in the hole on the right side of the Cooley line. It was the first meeting of the day between Currie and MacDonald.

"When I ran the ball I could feel a certain strength that I hadn't felt in any game before that," MacDonald said. "I still remember to this day how much stronger Currie was than anyone I played prior to that."

When St. Ambrose went back on offense, Currie slid inside to guard.

"We didn't know he was changing positions for the game," Cooley coach Roger Parmentier said. "How many coaches would change the position of their best player for the final game of the year?"

The St. Ambrose running game started clicking with Currie on the inside. D'Angelo ripped off a 25-yarder to the right. But Fournier dropped a long pass that could have gone for a touchdown. That left the Cavaliers in a punting situation at midfield.

Freshman Mike Goff gulped. He authored the bad center snap to Mike Cure on a punt in the Soup Bowl that almost proved disastrous against Shrine.

Punting team get ready to go, Boisture yelled.

"I was shaking in my boots," Goff said. "Here I'm 165 pounds and I'm going to have a guy 265 across from me. I was thinking I was going to have to snap the ball with Gus Kasapis throwing a forearm into my facemask.

"Then Tom says, 'O.K., punt team — Goff sit down, Currie center.' So I sat down on the bench and it was one of the warmest feelings I've ever had. I was never more relieved in my entire life. I wouldn't have to go snap against Kasapis. He could have picked me up and thrown me through the goalposts."

A 20-yard quarterback sweep by Bytnar moved Cooley to midfield but a sack by Currie and a dropped pass by Ken Barget left the Cardinals in a punting situation. Barget's short kick was returned 25 yards by Lantzy to midfield. But a 15-yard clipping penalty against the Cavaliers on the return moved the ball back to their own 20. If St. Ambrose was going to beat Cooley, it must first stop beating itself.

But Lamprides unloaded on the Cardinals again, this time completing a 32-yard pass to Henry Babisz. Lantzy then bolted 11 yards with one of those patented double handoffs in the Wing T, and D'Angelo popped an 11-yarder off right tackle.

St. Ambrose was again on Cooley's doorstep with a first down at the 11. Three more handoffs to D'Angelo produced a shocking

6-0 St. Ambrose lead. But Lamprides was sacked by MacDonald on his bootleg attempt for the conversion.

The St. Ambrose sideline was giddy.

"We found out they were flesh and blood just like us," Lantzy said. "We started picking up yards. The more we got into the game, the better we felt. We're thinking, 'We're not going to lose this ball game. We can beat these guys. They're not as big, tough and strong as everyone made them out to be.'"

But the glow didn't last long.

Two plays into Cooley's next possession, Bytnar rolled left and fired a 66-yard touchdown pass to Barget on a post pattern. The Cardinals then used every bit of their size and power to muscle open a hole for Kelley for the conversion run off tackle.

And that's the way the half ended — Cooley on top, 7-6.

"Those guys were so overconfident coming into the game — How could a school with 400 students play mighty Cooley?" Skip Paoletti said. "If we didn't have their attention in the first half, we certainly had it by the time the second half rolled around. Mike Currie was having a tremendous game. He was putting some real hits on their best players. They were surprised at how hard we could hit."

Cooley didn't look as big any more. The Cardinals looked lumbering. They were starting to slow down. The ball-handling of Lamprides was baffling them.

"If you didn't play your keys and stay in your lanes, they would kill you," Parmentier said. "That hurt us, because our kids were overly aggressive thinking they were going to murder these guys."

The Cavaliers were beating the Cardinals everywhere but on the scoreboard. But the previous week Eastern schooled Cooley in the first half of the PSL title game, only to see the Cardinals roar back in the second half for the victory.

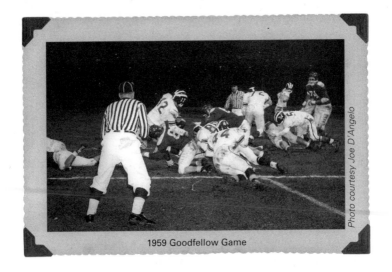

1959 Goodfellow Game

Photo courtesy Joe D'Angelo

The Cavaliers would need more than talent to stage this upset. They would need emotion. But there was no Knute Rockne halftime speech from Boisture, just a few words from the janitor.

"You guys have worked hard," John Tobianski told the players. "This may be the only chance you ever get. You've got 24 minutes to play. Make it your best 24 minutes."

The two teams engaged in a role reversal returning to the field in the second half. St. Ambrose was the team brimming with confidence, Cooley with doubt.

The assault on the statistics sheet continued. Lantzy returned the second half kickoff 35 yards to the Cooley 42, and the Cavaliers quickly moved to the 22 on the legs of Lantzy and D'Angelo. But center Ray DeVriendt left the game with pulled back muscles three plays into the half, turning Kasapis over to Federspiel. On a third-and-seven from the Cooley 22, a Lamprides pass for Currie was intercepted by Bytnar at the Cooley 1.

The Cardinals quick-kicked out of their end zone on third down but Bytnar's shank carried only 26 yards. Lamprides promptly caught Cooley in an eight-man front and threw a pass to a wide-open Henry Babisz in the end zone — but it sailed through his hands. So the Cavaliers turned back to the ground and marched to the Cooley 4 on runs by Cure, D'Angelo, and Fournier.

Facing a fourth-and-two, the Cavaliers went for it — but Lamprides' jump pass for Babisz bounced off his hands. Two second-half possessions, two wasted scoring opportunities.

Again Cooley couldn't dig itself out of the hole and again Parmentier ordered a quick kick. Again, the ploy backfired. Bytnar's line drive punt hit at the Cooley 30 and bounced back to the 21. But three plays later, on a sweep of left end from the Cooley 12, D'Angelo fumbled the ball away. Three second-half possessions, three blown scoring opportunities.

The game was now in the fourth quarter. Cooley had the ball and the lead. Time was running out on little St. Ambrose.

24

132 SPECIAL

St. Ambrose offensive backfield coach Bill David had been reminding Tom Boisture all game not to forget 132 Special. We put the play in specifically for this game, David figured, so why not run it?

But with the clock winding down in the fourth quarter, Boisture's mind was elsewhere. He was struggling with a dilemma. Mike Currie had the best hands on the team. He was St. Ambrose's best receiver. He already had a 33-yard catch in this game. The Cavaliers had dropped two passes that could have gone for touchdowns and already put this game away.

Only eight minutes remained in the Goodfellow game. Does Boisture return Currie to end where he could give the Cavaliers a chance for a big play? Or does he keep him in the interior line where his blocking would allow St. Ambrose to continue making the little plays?

Boisture decided to keep Currie inside where the once-intimidating Gus Kasapis seemed to be missing in action. Another short punt by Barget set the Cavaliers up at their own 46. Boisture sent his offense back onto the field with orders to do what the Cavaliers do best — run the football.

The Cardinals received a steady diet of Joe D'Angelo right, Larry Lantzy left, and Mike Cure up the middle. Three times the Cavaliers faced fourth downs in the drive and all three times the Cavaliers converted.

Cure powered his way up the gut for a first down on a fourth-and-1 at the Cooley 45. On a fourth-and-four at the Cooley 36

Manny Lamprides hit Henry Babisz on a jump pass across the middle for a seven-yard gain. The Cavaliers were munching up both yardage and clock.

But the third fourth down of the drive would determine the fate of David in this clash with Goliath. Ninety-two seconds remained and the Cavaliers found themselves in a fourth-and-3 at the Cooley 22.

St. Ambrose called a timeout, and Boisture mulled his options. Another jump pass? Lamprides completed both of his passes in the drive, which constituted a torrid streak for him. Another reverse to Lantzy? His speed had given the big Cooley defenders fits all night. D'Angelo again? The Cardinals were certain to be keying on him.

"I had a feeling it was going to be me," D'Angelo said. "I wanted the ball. Tom had come up with some surprises by throwing the ball on fourth downs. But maybe because we had dropped so many passes, he didn't want to risk this one. Sometimes as a coach you get the feel for a certain play at a certain time."

Boisture had a feel for 132 Special this time.

"They hadn't seen it," Boisture said. "They wouldn't recognize it. It put our best player out in front of our best running back."

In his bid to slay Goliath, Boisture would hand the slingshot to D'Angelo. Lamprides took the snap, Currie pulled, and D'Angelo ducked into a mass of bodies off right tackle in search of a first down to keep the drive — and dream — alive.

D'Angelo was met in the hole by Ted Bytnar and Doug Behnke. Currie and St. Ambrose right tackle Jim Conahan also were in the cluster of humanity. Ross MacDonald was closing fast from his defensive back position.

Time stood still.

"We came up and hit him and we were trying to drive him back," Cooley coach Roger Parmentier said. "I'm thinking, 'He's done.' But he was still moving his feet."

Before another heart could beat in all of Briggs Stadium, D'Angelo squirted loose. The pack was suddenly behind him and he was creating separation. Cooley linebacker Charles Rogers raced over in a last ditch effort to shove D'Angelo out of bounds. But he only got one hand on him — and D'Angelo sprinted the final 15 yards into the end zone untouched.

Pandemonium.

"I wasn't thinking touchdown," D'Angelo said. "I was thinking first down. What happened to me was luck in some ways. I got hit from so many different directions that I wasn't able to fall. I got hit by so many guys that it looked like I disappeared. They converged on me, everyone fell off — and I was left standing."

Boisture didn't even see the play. As the Cavaliers were lining up on fourth down, he was consulting his play sheet and telling fullback Mike Cure the next play in the event D'Angelo converted the first down.

"Then everyone started yelling and screaming," Boisture said.

He looked up and saw his offensive-line coach Bud Kurvink flapping his arms and bellowing, "He scored! He scored!"

Parmentier did see the play. Every last second of it.

"The referees claimed they never held him, that they never had a good grip on him," Parmentier said. "As I sit here 40-some years later, I cannot say if they did or did not. But I do know two of our guys had their arms on him."

Boisture quickly changed gears on the sideline, moving off a first-down call to a conversion play. This time he gave Lantzy the handoff and he beat the Cooley defenders to the left corner on a sweep, putting the Cavaliers up, 13-7.

Cooley would get the ball back with 1:20 remaining. But like St. Ambrose, the Cardinals were built to win games by running the football, not throwing it. Bytnar's second pass of the possession was intercepted by Lamprides and the biggest upset in Goodfellow history was sealed.

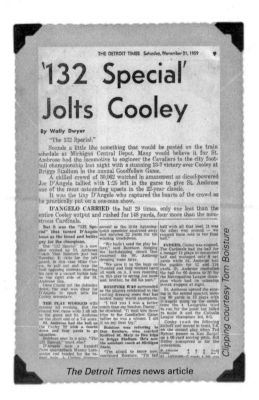

Clipping courtesy Tom Boisture

The Detroit Times news article

"It was an upset from the standpoint that my line averaged 230 and I had a fullback who was 210," Parmentier said. "But it wasn't an upset on the field. Better football players beat us."

St. Ambrose ran off 60 plays to Cooley's 30. The Cavaliers rushed for 208 yards and rolled up 294 total yards. The Cardinals gained only 144 yards [66 of them on one play] and managed just three first downs. In that frantic second half, St. Ambrose gained 121 yards on 31 plays. Cooley gained nine yards on 12 plays.

Parmentier was right in his initial assessment of St. Ambrose — the Cavaliers were a team that believed in its coach.

"We seemed to have it on our minds if we did everything the way we were coached, we couldn't lose," Lantzy said. "We were quick, we were deceptive and we had a couple monsters of our own on the line. We were running around them all night. They kind of ran out of gas. We literally wore them out.

"Boisture probably could have taken their team and beaten ours, and our team and beaten theirs."

D'Angelo finished the night with 148 yards on 29 carries — and finished the season with 1,268 yards on 99 carries with 17 touchdowns. The Cavaliers scored four touchdowns in two post-season games, all by D'Angelo.

"Joey was unbelievable," Mike Van Goethem said. "He's as tough as nails and as elusive as anyone I've ever seen. He wasn't the biggest or the fastest but in those first 40 yards he was hell on wheels."

After the game, the school with an enrollment of only 396 seemed to have 396 bodies in its locker room. Priests, fathers and brothers — Boisture's brother Dan, who would land Mike Currie as a recruit for Michigan State. Every Catholic in the city wanted to be a part of the celebration. The fathers of Lamprides and Bill Lenhard were ecstatic and emboldened by the Catholic school's stunning upset.

"They walked right down the tunnel into our locker room," Lenhard said. "As I was undressing, my father grabbed my helmet and told me, 'I'm taking your helmet.' So he walks off with it and wore it the entire night at the bar. Never took it off."

A couple of the Cavaliers also went out on the town looking for their doubters.

"Hal Schram likened us to David and Goliath," Ray Federspiel said. "That was a great motivator. After the game, a group of us went to the Free Press Building to speak with Mr. Hal Schram. He wasn't available, of course."

The next day, with the Cavaliers back on the East side, Boisture went back to work. He watched the game tape and finally got to see the winning touchdown. It was celluloid justification of his decision to feature D'Angelo in this offense — that ability to escape.

St. Ambrose first Goodfellow win – 1959

Photo courtesy Jim Conahan

Left side: Cooley Co-Captains Ross MacDonald and Larry Scroby; Right side: St. Ambrose Co-Captains Jim Conahan and Vince Taormino.
Photo by *Detroit News*

"They could have blown the whistle," Boisture said. "Looking at the film, he did get hit and he did stop. But it was second effort. When he got hit, if they thought he was going to get killed and blown the whistle, it would have been justified. The guy had the whistle in his mouth. You could see it on tape...Joey came to a standstill but it was STOP (clapping his hands) — then POP. That's where the quickness came in. That's why he was such a good player — that quickness."

Boisture wasn't the only person in the St. Ambrose locker room in the dungeon of the school anxious to see that play.

"We ran that film 100 times," Lenhard said, "and we still wondered how he got out of there."

"Probably Catholic officials," mused MacDonald decades later.

25

GOODFELLOW 2

Tom Boisture eagerly awaited the start of the 1960 season. His St. Ambrose Cavaliers were the city champions in 1959 and figured to be even better the next year. His all-state halfback Joe D'Angelo was returning. So were Manny Lamprides, Larry Lantzy, and Bill Fournier. All would be a year older, a year better.

But first Boisture would have to answer for his sins. Father David Weisner, the school's athletic director, was summoned downtown by the Detroit Catholic League.

"We got turned in after the Goodfellow Game," Boisture said. "Servite, I would guess, for Mike Currie's transfer, for illegal practices. So Father Weisner had to go in front of the committee. He was catching all kinds of hell.

"He came back and said, 'Tom, you can't practice in the hall any more. You just can't.' Father Weisner was putting the heat on me. During basketball season he'd come over to the gym just to make sure we were practicing basketball. But John [Tobianski] worked it out where Father wouldn't be around when he didn't need to be."

One of those days was Ascension Thursday. Catholics believe Jesus Christ rose from the dead (Easter) and then ascended into heaven 40 days later (Ascension). So the Church declares such feasts as Christmas, the Immaculate Conception, and the Ascension holy days of obligation — and Catholic schools never hold class on holy days.

1961 City Championship Offense

Offensive line (l to r): Mike Goff, Don Emch, Dave Vitali, Marshall Houle, Bill Lenhard, Jack Cairo, Chuck Kuess; Offensive backfield: Pete Genord, Ron Albers, Ray Malcoun, Mike VanGoethem; Coach: Tom Boisture

Boisture thought the Feast of the Ascension would be an opportune time to take his team on a picnic. So he gathered the Cavaliers that Wednesday in May and delivered the good news.

"The Dad's Club sold some extra tickets," Boisture said. "As a reward before the season starts, we're going on a picnic. Don't worry about anything. Don't bring anything. We'll bring all the food and punch. We're going to have fun and develop some camaraderie."

"Can we bring dates?" one player asked.

"No, don't bring dates," Boisture said. "All that has been taken care of."

Boisture told the players the picnic would be at the Irish Hills, a vacation spot 90 miles west of Detroit and south of Jackson. It was a postcard-type resort area with rolling hills and lakes. Boisture entertained his team with stories of how he went on picnics there as a kid with his brother, sister and their friends.

Boisture was showing some rare compassion to his team.

"So we're all bright-eyed," Pete Piazza said. "It's a nice hot day and we're going on a picnic. Sweet deal. But when we get to school all we heard was, 'Go to your locker, grab the bag in front of it and put it on the bus.' The bag had every piece of equipment you owned."

"You never know when another team might show up," Boisture said.

The school's two maroon and white busses both traveled to the picnic. The players were in one, their equipment in the other. It took almost 2 ½ hours for the school's chug-a-lug busses to reach Irish Hills.

"It took forever," Skip Paoletti said. "To this day I have no idea where the Irish Hills are."

There were another two busses already there when the Cavaliers arrived. Lo and behold, the Salesian High football team also was on a picnic that day. And the Knights also brought their equipment. Frank Buford, who worked the Goodfellow Game in the press box for St. Ambrose, was the Salesian coach.

"It was about 900 degrees," Mike Van Goethem said. "It was hot and dusty and not anywhere near the picnic we were promised."

So the Cavaliers and Knights suited up for battle. There was one problem — John Tobianski forgot to pack any chinstraps.

"They had to tape our helmets to our heads," Tom Beer said.

Then the two sides went at it — far, far away from the watchful eyes of the Catholic League.

"It was amazing that we never got caught," Piazza said. "I don't know what Tom was thinking. I don't know what the Salesian coach was thinking. We played a game. No, it was worse than a game because there weren't any timeouts and there was no half-time. It was play, play, play, and play. It was hot and we scrimmaged all day. There were little slopes here and there. I remember knocking down passes as I was running down hills."

After the scrimmage, the players were given a brief liberty by Boisture.

"We jumped into this little river there to wash ourselves off," Beer said. "It was hot — especially with your helmet taped to your head."

There was one casualty. When the Cavaliers returned to Grosse Pointe, D'Angelo developed mononucleosis.

"I was in the hospital for almost a week," he said. "I think God was trying to tell me something."

Boisture certainly wasn't listening. He loved to scrimmage. During his tenure as the head coach at St. Ambrose, he arranged scrimmages against Riverview and its all-state quarterback Lloyd Carr, who would go on to become the head coach at Michigan. Boisture arranged scrimmages against Hamtramck and its all-state running back Dewey Lincoln, who would go on to play at Michigan State. Boisture always lined up bigger Class A opponents for his Class C school.

"Tom would always get schools he thought could be better than us," Bill Fournier said. "We'd go against these teams and run the same play 10, 12 times in a row. You're going full contact and they know it's coming — and Tom wants them to know. It's hard to block somebody when they know what's coming. It was frustrating because you knew you were going to get nailed.

"But when we got into our season we knew by halftime we were going to take a team out. You could be down, even or a touchdown up. But we just knew we were better than they were."

Boisture scheduled one scrimmage too many in 1960. The irony was that scrimmage against Grand Rapids South was legal. It was one of two allowed by the Catholic League during the official window of fall practice.

"We thought we were so smart," Boisture said. "But it was a long way, a long way. It was terrible. A lot of things happened. It was like a Super Bowl for them."

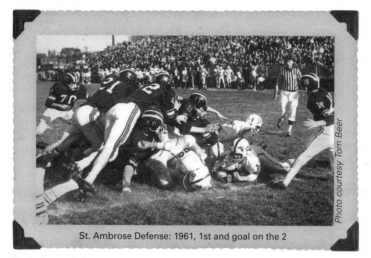

St. Ambrose Defense: 1961, 1st and goal on the 2

Photo courtesy Tom Beer

St. Ambrose defense stopped Redford St. Mary's offense on 4 straight attempts to score.

Start with the bus ride. The most direct route from Detroit to Grand Rapids in 1960 was straight out Grand River Avenue. That constituted a 125-mile trip with stoplights...and no air conditioning.

"It had to be 980 degrees that day," Skip Paoletti said. "So up Grand River we go. About halfway there, one of the busses conked out."

Luckily, the St. Ambrose caravan was in East Lansing at the time. While the overheated bus was being serviced, the players walked across the street to a restaurant to buy hamburgers for 15 cents.

"It was the first time any of us had ever seen a McDonald's," Paoletti said.

After a few hours, the bus was repaired and the Cavaliers again loaded up to continue the longest journey of their lives.

"When we get there, we're exhausted," Paoletti said. "We've been on the bus for 8-9 hours, so they pushed the scrimmage back from afternoon to evening. We get dressed in the locker room and come out to warm up. The lights are on and there are 6,000-7,000 people there to watch.

"By beating Cooley, we allowed Grand Rapids Catholic Central to win the state championship. Everyone wanted to see what this little tiny Catholic school that beat Cooley was all about."

The travel took its toll on Lamprides. He was sick and didn't play. D'Angelo also wished he hadn't played. He suffered a sprained ankle that would cost him the chance to repeat his double as an all-city, all-state running back.

"That knocked my pins out," D'Angelo said. "Even though I played every game that season, I didn't have the mobility or the speed I had my junior year. I could never get my ankle to heal."

The Catholic League realigned in 1960. It already had a powerful sector of all-boys schools that included Catholic Central, DeLaSalle, Notre Dame, and the University of Detroit. That was dubbed the Red division. The Catholic League also created a super division of co-ed schools, lumping St. Ambrose with Benedictine, Redford St. Mary, Servite, Shrine, St. Anthony, and St. Catherine. That became the White division.

Shrine, with Al Fracassa in his first year as coach, avenged its Soup Bowl loss to St. Ambrose, 33-19, in the third week of the 1960 season. John Seymour produced touchdowns rushing, receiving and throwing for the Knights that night. St. Mary also whipped St. Ambrose, 26-13, two weeks later. The Cavaliers failed to defend their city and Catholic titles with a 5-3 record.

But Lamprides was finally rewarded for his three-year contribution to St. Ambrose, earning all-city honors at quarterback.

"Tom always said he had his best talent in 1960," Marshall Houle said. "He was very disappointed they didn't win the championship that year. He said his big mistake was being too cautious. He didn't want anyone to get hurt. So he came out the next year blazing. You played full speed all the time. Either you got hurt or you didn't. We never had an injury."

The 1960 Cavaliers depended on their runners. The 1961 Cavaliers would pin their hopes on the blockers. Returning starters Jack Cairo, Bill Lenhard, and Dave Vitali would all be seniors. So would co-captain Don Emch at the other tackle.

There was youth everywhere else. Talented youth. That 1959 recruiting class of Ron Albers, Tom Beer, Pete Genord, Mike Goff, Marshall Houle, Chuck Kuess, Ray Malcoun, Pete Piazza, Cory Richardson, and Mike Van Goethem had physically matured and was assuming greater responsibilities on the field.

"I knew we had a good group of sophomore and juniors coming up, players who were dedicated," Beer said. "I knew we had the talent. All we needed to do was put it together."

St. Ambrose survived the opener against Benedictine, 7-6, when Beer blocked an extra point kick by the Ravens. That was the only close game the Cavaliers played all season. But not the most important game. In a clash of old and new powers, Redford St. Mary and St. Ambrose took matching 5-0 records into their game at McCabe Field. Jack Clancy, who would go on to play for Michigan and the Miami Dolphins, was the St. Mary star. But he didn't star that day. Ray Malcoun did, rushing for touchdowns of 49, 13, and 3 yards as the Cavaliers prevailed, 21-6.

"They had good players," Beer said. "But we always outschemed teams. Boisture was a real genius. We didn't make any mistakes and when the other team did, we capitalized. That was the key to our success. We weren't bigger, stronger or faster than other teams. We were just better prepared."

A 7-0 record gave the Cavaliers the White division title and earned them a Soup Bowl date with Catholic Central. It was no contest. The Cavaliers destroyed the defending Catholic League champions, 37-0, in front of a crowd of 18,479. Denny Peternal

MVP Tom Beer, as a Denver Bronco

Photo courtesy Tom Beer

intercepted two passes, returning one for a 17-yard touchdown, to win game MVP honors.

"They weren't in our class," Beer said. "We totally outplayed 'em, outfinessed 'em, outpowered 'em. They had some good players, but they just didn't have the athletes to compete with us."

That earned the Cavaliers a second trip to the Goodfellow Game to play the Pershing Doughboys. Houle, for one, was disappointed. He was hoping to play defending city champion Denby, another East side school.

"They were unbeaten," Houle said, "but somehow Pershing wound up in the Goodfellow Game. They didn't even play Denby. They said if Denby and St. Ambrose had played, there might have been 50,000 people at the game. Briggs Stadium would have been packed for St. Ambrose-Denby."

Still, a record Goodfellow Game crowd of 39,196 turned out at Tiger Stadium — the name was changed from "Briggs" that year — to see the Cavaliers blank Pershing, 20-0. That crowd also witnessed one of the most spectacular defensive plays in the history of the Goodfellow Game — a play that would earn Beer game MVP honors.

As a junior, Beer was emerging as the school's most versatile player since Mike Currie. He also was the best athlete St. Ambrose had ever seen. He would letter in hockey, basketball, baseball and track. He received all-city honors in both basketball and baseball in his prep career, and the St. Louis baseball Cardinals offered him a contract out of high school.

In football, Beer was listed as a quarterback and saw the field in short yardage and goal-line situations. But he was a dynamo at inside linebacker, just like Currie.

Jack Cairo lined up in front of Beer on defense at tackle, and the two would run their own stunts. If Beer tapped Cairo on the butt once, he wanted Cairo to charge the right gap. Then Beer would fill the left gap. If Beer tapped him twice, Cairo would go left and Beer right.

Trailing 6-0 midway through the second quarter, Pershing drove to midfield. Beer inched up to the line and tapped Cairo once on the behind. Beer wanted Cairo to fill the right gap.

"But at the last minute, I don't know why — fate, I guess — I tapped him on the ass a second time," Beer said. "So Jack looped out and I crashed inside."

Beer raced untouched into the backfield where Bill Lenhard's shoulder was already planted in quarterback George Richardson's backside as he attempted to hand off to fullback Bob Engel. The ball popped into the air. Beer never broke stride for a 47-yard touchdown.

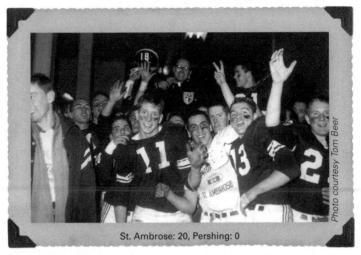

St. Ambrose: 20, Pershing: 0

Photo courtesy Tom Beer

Celebrating in locker room at Tiger Stadium 1961 Goodfellow City Championship.

"I saw it, grabbed it, and ran like hell," Beer said. "I scored before anyone knew what happened. All because of a last-second change of a stunt. It made my career."

St. Ambrose prevailed in a game that wasn't as close as the score indicates. Pershing managed only five first downs and turned the ball over eight times on five fumbles and three interceptions.

Pershing's all-state center Tom Cecchini would go on to serve as a captain at the University of Michigan in 1965. Pershing defensive back Ted Sizemore went on to became the National League Rookie of the Year in 1969 as a second baseman with the Los Angeles Dodgers.

St. Ambrose had three all-state blockers on the field in the 1961 Goodfellow Game: seniors Jack Cairo, Bill Lenhard, and Dave Vitali. Cairo was named by the *Detroit News*, Lenhard by the *Detroit Free Press*, and Vitali by the Associated Press. Lenhard also became the school's second All-America.

All three players left after the season. They would have company walking out the door.

CHANGE

Tom Boisture wasn't the only football coach recruiting in the winter of 1962.

Bill Yeoman left Michigan State to become the head coach at the University of Houston in 1962. He hired Chuck Fairbanks, another member of the Michigan State Mafia, to be an assistant. With a brother coaching at Michigan State and his best player (Mike Currie) in East Lansing, Boisture was an honorary member of that Mafia. The Godfather, Duffy Daugherty, had written a letter of recommendation to St. Ambrose that helped Boisture get hired. Boisture didn't have green blood, but he was close.

Larry Lantzy was already on the Houston campus and Yeoman wanted Boisture to join him, springing the offer for Tom to become an assistant coach during a February recruiting trip. With two city championships in three years, Boisture knew the time was right to take the next step in his coaching career.

Fr. David Weisner, the school's athletic director, was upset with the news that he was losing his football coach. But he moved quickly to fill the vacancy. Within a day of Boisture's disclosure, Fr. Weisner contacted Redford St. Mary coach Nick Galante. This would be a one-candidate, one-interview hire.

But Boisture wasn't out the door yet. Nor was he off the hook. He received a phone call from the Godfather.

"What are the chances of getting George Perles the job at St. Ambrose?" Daugherty asked Boisture.

"That might be tough," Boisture said. "They're already talking to the Redford St. Mary coach and are about to hire him. Let me check it out, though."

Daugherty suggested that Boisture contact Perles, another member of the Michigan State Mafia, who at the time was an assistant high-school coach at Catholic League power St. Rita in Chicago. Boisture knew Perles from his old west-side neighborhood. He was two years behind Boisture at Western High before attending Michigan State.

So Boisture phoned Perles.

"George was kind of blasé about it," Boisture said. "Then I told him Duffy called and told me to get him the job — and I just wanted to make sure he wanted it."

Boisture didn't want to let Daugherty down. Neither did Perles.

"I didn't know how I was going to pull this off," Boisture said. "I was upset and nervous about it."

So Boisture went to the resident answer man at St. Ambrose — John Tobianski.

"I've got a problem," Boisture told the janitor.

"What — you're not taking the Houston job?" Tobianski said.

"No," Boisture said. "Duffy called me and wants to get George Perles the job. For St. Ambrose, this is the guy. With his background, he'd be ideal for you. You'll love him."

"If you say he's O.K., we're going to get him the job," Tobianski said.

"How are you going to do that?" Boisture asked. "Fr. Weisner loves the other guy."

"Don't worry about Fr. Weisner," Tobianski said. "I'll take care of him."

So Tobianski walked across the street to the rectory for a visit with St. Ambrose parish pastor Fr. Francis Van Antwerp.

A short time later, Boisture received a phone call.

Photo courtesy Dave Brozo/Gari Michaels

George Perles

"You tell Duffy that George has the job," Tobianski said.

In a span of two hours Tobianski became an honorary member of the Michigan State Mafia as well.

"John had Father Van wrapped around his finger because he did as much for the parish — the buildings and the grounds — as he did for the football team," Boisture said.

Daugherty had placed Perles at St. Rita in 1960 because he wanted to beef up his recruiting in the Chicago area. He sent Larry Bielat, another former Spartan, along with Perles to serve as an assistant. In their one year there, St. Rita reached the Catholic League championship game at Soldier Field.

But with talent suddenly spewing at St. Ambrose, Daugherty decided he needed Perles closer to home. Perles would become the head football coach and Bielat would assist him. Daugherty sweetened the deal for Bielat, telling him the two could switch positions in the winter — Bielat would be the head basketball coach with Perles his assistant.

"George admitted to me that he didn't know much about basketball," Bielat said. "So I told him, 'George, you just sit down at the end of the bench and keep the towels folded.' He said, 'I'm not going to do that.'"

There was one hitch. Perles accepted his new position over the telephone. When Perles and Bielat drove across Michigan to report for work at St. Ambrose, it was the first time either had seen the school and its facilities. Or lack thereof.

"We're coming from St. Rita, which was an all-boys school in Chicago with 2,000 kids," Bielat said. "We show up at St. Ambrose and there are 400 kids, including 200 girls. We didn't have a football stadium. We didn't have a practice field. We didn't have a home court in basketball.

"I didn't know how Tom had done it. I just assumed he must have been real hard up for a job."

So Boisture was out, Perles in. Boisture left behind the greatest team St. Ambrose would ever field.

27

BEST

George Perles and Larry Bielat both needed summer jobs to supplement their paltry teaching/coaching salaries from St. Ambrose. So Perles landed work as the gatekeeper at Grosse Pointe Park's municipal park on Windmill Pointe Drive, and Bielat found work in construction.

"George would sit in this little shack and let people in," Bielat said. "On days it rained, we didn't work in construction. So I'd drive over to the yacht club, park next to the shack and and we'd sit in there talking football — 'Here's how we're going to teach this, here's how we're going to run that.'

"Cars would be pulling in and George would just be waving them through. I'd say, 'George, you don't even know if those folks belong.' He'd say, 'Ah, we're working.' We'd be arguing over things and all of a sudden George would look at his watch and say, 'Damn, I should have left two hours ago.'"

But before Perles and Bielat could become game-planners, they would need to become salesmen. These two young men — Perles was 28, Bielat 24 — needed to sell a city championship football team that they knew what they were doing as coaches.

"It was a shock to us when Boisture moved on," Ray Malcoun said. "Who was this guy coming in from Chicago? Any time you have a new coach there's some trepidation. With a new coach comes a new system. Hey, we had a great thing going. We were winning a lot of football games. Who is this guy…and what's it all going to mean?

"But we still had John Tobianski."

Perles met Tobianski upon his arrival in Grosse Pointe but didn't realize how instrumental he was in his hiring. Tobianski, after all, was the school janitor. But Perles figured it all out in August when practice began.

"We'd have meetings after practice and George and I would go back into the coal bin and close the door," Bielat said. "Tobianski would come in. At first we'd look at each other and say, ` What the hell is the janitor doing here?' Then you found out how important this guy was to the community — and what a great judge of character he was.

"He'd be sitting there and George and I would be talking about a particular play. All of a sudden Tobianski would say, 'I know you don't want to hear what I've got to say — but you're going to listen.' George and I would look at each other and he'd continue, 'That son of a bitch is loafing. If you don't think he's loafing, you guys have been busy watching everybody else. I'm watching him. Last year he played a lot better than he is right now and if you don't get on his ass, he's going to be loafing on you all season.' We'd look at him and say, 'Damn, John, that's pretty astute.'

"The next morning before class we'd have that kid down in the coal bin telling him, 'You know what? We hear you played a lot harder and a lot better last year. What the hell's the problem? If you don't straighten things out, you're not only going to be off the team, you're going to be out of St. Ambrose.' We'd use those kind of scare tactics."

There was never a problem with Tom Beer in practice or in games. He was a special athlete — and Perles came to appreciate him as a special person.

During two-a-days at Defer before the start of the season, the Cavaliers were having problems blocking. With four starting offensive linemen gone from the 1961 team, inexperience was rampant up front. Perles was having trouble with one particular guard executing his assignments in All-America Bill Lenhard's old spot.

"He was making mistake after mistake," Beer said, "and Perles kept screaming and screaming. So I said, 'Coach, let me play there.' I knew I wasn't going to be the quarterback. Ron (Albers) was a good ball-handler and a good passer, just a good all-around athlete. I was starting on defense and a co-captain. But I wanted to play 48 minutes, not just go one way."

So Perles plugged the lanky Beer in at guard — just as Boisture had plugged his best player in at guard in the 1959 Goodfellow Game. Suddenly, the offensive line stabilized. And the only mystery on the 1962 team had been solved.

That recruiting class of 1959 was finally ready to carve out its own identity. For three years it watched and learned how to become champions. Now seniors, the St. Ambrose tradition was squarely on their shoulders.

"It was that mindset you grew up with as a freshman and a sophomore," Mike Van Goethem said. "You were expected to win, you were expected to be the best.

"It wasn't a question of whether we were going to win, but how much were we going to win by...or whether we were going to shut the other team out. That was the way you were measured. It was, 'I know you won, but it was only 20-0.' We were expected to win big. That was the prevailing attitude."

In a span of four years, Tom Beer transformed himself into Mike Currie. Van Goethem had become Joe D'Angelo. Pete Genord had become Larry Lantzy. Ron Albers had become Manny Lamprides. Ray Malcoun had become Vince Taormino. Mike Goff had become Henry Babisz. Cory Richardson had become Jim Conahan.

Except better.

Perles would make some changes from the Boisture way. The Wing T was out.

Photo courtesy Ray Malcoun

1962 coaches and offensive backfield

Coaches: Larry Bielat, George Perles
Players: Ron Albers, Pete Genord, Mike
VanGoethem, Ray Malcoun

"Tom ran double reverses and a lot of complicated, gimmicky plays," Perles said. "I couldn't duplicate that, so I went to a Full House backfield and we pounded away. His offense was beautiful — finesse with a lot of imagination. But I didn't feel comfortable doing that. We were very conservative. We just ran it and ran it and ran it. There's more than one way to skin a cat."

And pound on the Catholic teams the Cavaliers did, both on offense and defense. St. Ambrose opened the season with four consecutive shutouts, whipping Holy Redeemer (21-0), Benedictine (34-0), St. Anthony (34-0), and Servite (32-0).

Shrine also took a 4-0 record and a string of three consecutive shutouts into a showdown match with St. Ambrose. The Knights, with their all-state quarterback Chuck Lowther, scored the game's first touchdown.

"I remember one of the Shrine players taunting us, saying, 'We scored on the great St. Ambrose,'" Albers said. "But Tom Beer blocked the extra point and it was a total rout after that. We dominated the whole game."

St. Ambrose prevailed, 25-6. Shrine unveiled a single wing offense that night but the Cavaliers were ready for it.

"There was a lay teacher at St. Ambrose who knew someone who taught at Shrine," Beer said. "The Shrine players were all excited that week because Al Fracassa was putting in a single wing to beat us. The teacher told Perles and we shut them down.

"That was supposed to be their big surprise. But teachers talking to teachers talking to the coaches....We put in some basic stuff to defend the single wing and the rest is history."

St. Ambrose allowed another touchdown the next week against Dearborn Sacred Heart. The Cavaliers led just 7-6 at halftime.

"Sacred Heart never should have scored on us," Beer said. "They were a bad team. But you can't be up for every game. It was our homecoming and we knew we were going to beat them. Perles was so livid at halftime — you could see the paint curling off the walls.

"We came out in the second half and scored on them — and kept scoring on them. We should have allowed only the one touchdown in the regular season by Shrine."

The Cavaliers prevailed, 48-6, as Pete Genord produced the greatest half of football ever by a Cavalier. He scored touchdowns the first four times he touched the ball in the second half on runs of 60, 55, 49 and 47 yards. Typical Perles, he kept calling the same play — Fly 139 — until Sacred Heart could stop it. Genord finished the night with eight carries for 209 yards.

Perles expected discipline from his players, and the school expected discipline from its students.

St. Ambrose enforced a dress code — the boys wore sports coats and ties and the girls wore uniforms with knee-length plaid skirt, white blouse, and green blazer. There was a zero tolerance policy. Jim Laskowski was supposed to be the captain of the 1959 Goodfellow champions but was kicked out of school that spring for his repeated and open defiance of the dress code.

"I wore the same tie for four years," Goff said.

St. Ambrose did offer one day of freedom each week in the fall for a select few. On Fridays, the football team was allowed to wear its letter sweaters and the cheerleaders allowed to wear their game-night garb. The school day would conclude with the student body trooping over to the hall for a pep rally. The cheerleaders would stage skits and lead cheers, and the football captains would speak of their task that weekend.

"The pep rallies were the coolest things," quarterback Ron Albers said. "The players would make a grand entrance, all in our letter sweaters, and the place would be rocking."

"It was more noise than your ears could handle," added Pete Piazza. "We were always winning so it was always exciting."

The pep rallies were growing louder by the week in 1962.

St. Ambrose closed the regular season with a 28-0 victory over Redford St. Mary. That sent them into the Soup Bowl against Notre Dame with an 16-game winning streak.

Then came the most entertaining moment of the season for the Cavaliers. At practice, of all places.

Tom Boisture was always paranoid about opponents spying on the Cavaliers because of the openness of Defer. Only a chain link fence stood between any set of eyes and a St. Ambrose practice.

The Cavaliers were practicing at midweek, and one of the players committed a mental error. So Perles told him to take a lap

Varsity cheerleaders

Photo courtesy Tom Beer

around Defer. At the conclusion of his jaunt, the player went directly to Perles.

"Hey coach, as I was taking my lap I saw a guy sitting in a car," he said. "He's got a notepad. He's watching our practices and taking notes."

Perles turned eight shades of red.

"That son of a bitch," Perles said. "He's spying on us."

So Perles told Bielat to run practice, that he was going to go catch a spy.

"You have to understand George is a really tough, street-fighting guy," Bielat said. "So he sneaks off behind the building, down the block, around the corner and all of a sudden he comes up behind this guy in his car parked by the fence."

"What are you doing?" Perles screamed, then reached into the car, grabbed the spy by the collar and yanked him bodily out the driver's side window. "I'm going to kick the shit out of you."

By now all the Cavaliers are standing on the field watching their coach administer his own brand of justice.

"The guy actually peed in his pants," Bielat said. "We're all standing there watching his pants getting wet."

"Who put you up to this — Bazylewicz?" Perles screamed.

Perles grabbed the guy's notepad, ripped it up and threw it in the air. Then he reached in the car, grabbed the keys and heaved them onto the roof of a house.

"Get out of here," Perles said.

"Off the guy goes, walking down the street with no car and wet pants," Bielat said.

Perles was scheduled to appear on the Van Patrick television show the next night with Notre Dame coach Walt Bazylewicz as a prelude to the Soup Bowl. When the Cavaliers returned to school after practice, Perles phoned Bazylewicz.

"I caught your guy watching practice today," Perles said.

"What are you talking about?" the Notre Dame coach said.

"I was going to kick the shit out of him, but he wet his pants just like a little girl," Perles said. "But I'm going to see you tomorrow and I'm going to kick your ass. It's going to be the best fight television has ever seen — right in front of Van Patrick."

Perles slammed the phone down. But there would be no fight.

"George was a real gentleman on TV that night," Bielat said. "But before the show he and Walt really got into it verbally. Walt kept denying it."

Perles continued to simmer. He wanted his team to share in his rage. So on Thursday, on the eve of the Soup Bowl, Perles and Bielat were in the coal bin discussing motivational tactics.

"What can we do to get the team really excited?" Perles asked Bielat.

Notre Dame's colors were green and white, so Perles said, "Let's paint the door to our locker room."

That evening Perles and Bielet went to a local hardware store and bought cans of green and white paint. They waited until the dead of night — midnight — when all was quiet and dark.

"So here's George and I sneaking over there, slapping paint on the door, half green and half white," Bielat said.

The next morning, when the players reported to school, always through the locker-room door, they were irate.

"Holy mackerel, coach, did you see what those damn guys from Notre Dame did to our door?" one said.

"No, no...we didn't," Perles said. So Perles and Bielat trooped out back and stood at the top of the stairs leading down to the locker-room door and the basement of the school.

"Can you believe those guys painted our door?" the players said.

Bielat looked down at Perles' shoes and saw splotches of green paint on them.

"Coach," Bielat whispered, "you'd better sneak into the locker room and put your tennis shoes on. You're a horrible painter."

Much like Tobianski's chicken ploy before the 1956 Soup Bowl, the Perles door trick didn't work.

Under the direction of quarterback Dave Bonior, Notre Dame took a 13-12 lead over St. Ambrose by halftime before a record Soup Bowl crowd of 20,112 at the University of Detroit stadium. Bonior would go on to serve as the Democratic whip in the U.S. House of Representatives from 1991-2002. Randy Lamprides, the younger brother of Manny, also was in the Irish backfield that night. Both Notre Dame touchdowns were gift-wrapped by St. Ambrose fumbles in its own end.

"We were shocked," Pete Piazza said. "We couldn't believe that we were losing. Losing wasn't something we understood. I can remember that locker room being very quiet, very somber. I remember the silence. I remembered coming out — we were of a conviction that that was it, no more. We were going to find a way to win...and we did."

Photo courtesy Mike Goff

St. Ambrose first TD against Cooley on long pass play

Mike Goff 42 on the ground after catching Ron Albers 30 yard pass over 3 Cooley defenders from St. Ambrose first touchdown just before halftime. St. Ambrose leads 6-0 at halftime.
Photo by *Detroit News*

The Cavaliers in general and Mike Van Goethem in particular found the way. Van Goethem fumbled away his first carry of the night, which allowed Notre Dame to take a 7-0 lead. But he scored on a 59-yard sprint later in the first quarter and runs of 7, 2 and 1 in the second half to power the Cavaliers to a 33-13 triumph and capture game MVP honors. Van Goethem rushed 25 times for 174 yards. Goff, a grade-school teammate of Bonior at St. Veronica, intercepted the Notre Dame quarterback twice and the Fighting Irish gained five total yards in the second half.

That delivered St. Ambrose a rematch in the Goodfellow Game against Cooley. The Cardinals earned the PSL championship with 25-6 drubbing of Denby, which ended the Tars' 27-game winning streak.

But it was no longer David and Goliath. The St. Ambrose enrollment swelled over 500 students and the Cavaliers were now competing as a Class B school. They went into the game ranked

No. 2 in that classification. Cooley, with an 8-0 record including five shutouts, was ranked No. 3 in Class A.

"We were cocky little boys back then," Piazza said. "We thought we could go down to Wayne State and take them on."

The entire program was cocky. John Tobianski drove downtown to Tiger Stadium that week to inspect the field, then informed on-site officials that it was not up to St. Ambrose's standards. Good enough for the NFL Detroit Lions, maybe, but not the Cavaliers.

The fourth largest crowd in Goodfellow history turned out at Tiger Stadium — 37,763. But the Cardinals couldn't out-finesse the Cavaliers in 1959 and couldn't overpower them in 1962. St. Ambrose gave the city a taste of George Perles football.

"We started the game off with an eight-man line, a goal-line type of offense," Perles said. "We ran a wham the first eight plays of the game just to get the kids settled down and relaxed, to get rid of the jitters of playing at Tiger Stadium."

Van Goethem remembers that series well. He carried the ball on every one of those eight power smashes.

"I got back to the huddle for the ninth play and told Albers, 'Give the God damn ball to Genord. They're killing me. I'm not running it any more,'" Van Goethem said. "Their linebackers were just waiting for me. But that was Perles. If you didn't stop it, it was coming at you again. When you finally stopped it, he'd try something else."

Twenty-five years later, as the head coach at Michigan State, Perles ordered up 56 handoffs to Lorenzo White in a game against Indiana. If he had a great back, Perles was going to feature him. Van Goethem was a great back — and these Cavaliers were a great team. They rolled over Cooley, 19-0, to capture another city and state title. Roger Parmentier fell to 0-2 against St. Ambrose in Goodfellow Games.

Remember Mike Goff, who gratefully took a seat as a freshman in the 1959 Goodfellow game? Now a senior, Goff caught a

30-yard touchdown pass from Ron Albers in the final minute of the first half to give St. Ambrose a 6-0 lead. Van Goethem took it from there, rushing 33 times for 165 yards and the other two touchdowns. St. Ambrose outscored the opposition, 274-25, on the season.

"It's not that we had any spectacular individual talent," Piazza said. "For some reason Tom Beer got a lot of individual accolades. He did well, made it to the pros, so maybe he was spectacular. But we didn't look at him as anything special. He was a good football player. But Mike Van Goethem was a good football player. Albers was a good football player. We were all good football players.

"We didn't have a LeBron James on our team. We all fell into sync with each other and worked very well as a team. We had a lot of pride in what we did. We didn't have any superstars. We had 11 guys on both sides of the ball who played very well together. Everyone watched out for each other and covered for each other."

But Perles was focusing on the 1963 season even before the Cavaliers took the field for their final game of 1962. Football season may come to an end, but the recruiting season never ends. Perles invited a handful of eighth graders from around the East side to attend the Goodfellow Game as his guest and brought them down to the locker room afterward. They would be the diamonds in the next class of greatness at St. Ambrose — and this night was the trump card Perles was playing in their recruitment.

"Those guys were bigger than life: Sam Bouhanna, Vince Locricchio, Mike Goff, Ray Malcoun, Mike Van Goethem," said Greg Hacias, a quarterback from Our Lady Queen of Heaven. "In the mind of an eighth-grade kid, these guys are legends. They were like NFL superstars or Michael Jordan to us kids. I couldn't sleep for weeks."

Van Goethem rushed for 1,045 yards and scored 19 touchdowns in 1962 to earn all-state honors. Beer also earned all-state

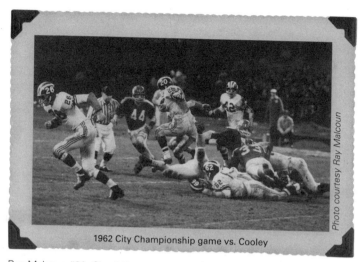

1962 City Championship game vs. Cooley

Ray Malcoun #20, Chuck Kuess #26, Greg Bringard #62, Mike Goff #42, Steve Himburg #66.

honors and became the school's third All-America. Van Goethem accepted a scholarship to Michigan State and Beer to Notre Dame, although he would finish at the University of Houston through the University of Detroit. Beer became a second-round draft pick of the Denver Broncos and played six NFL seasons.

Perles busted his tail to get his players scholarships.

"Perles called me out of class one day to visit with the defensive coordinator from the University of Buffalo," Mike Goff said. "So I went down to the coal bin and met with Buddy Ryan."

A week after the Goodfellow Game, Van Goethem and Goff were feature performers in a St. Ambrose senior class play, "No More Homework." Chuck Kuess handled the curtain that night and Malcoun served as a stage hand for the production.

This senior class did it all, on the field and off.

PERLES

George Perles was embracing the St. Ambrose way. In particular, the Dad's Club dollars.

The more the Cavaliers won, the more the money poured in.

"The Dad's Club was raising $1,500 a month," Perles said. "They raised about $18,000 a year so we could have all the things we wanted."

Perles would move the team postseason banquets to the Knights of Columbus Hall and pump up the guest list: Lions owner William Clay Ford and his Hall of Fame linebacker Joe Schmidt, Pro Bowlers Dan Currie and Ron Kramer from the Green Bay Packers, Duffy Daugherty…everyone seemed willing to celebrate the glory of St. Ambrose.

"Our banquet was something special," Perles said. "When it was over, we'd clear the kids out and have drinks, a band, and a party for the Dad's Club."

Like his predecessor Tom Boisture, Perles became close to Jay Louwers, the representative from Griswold Sports, the city's largest athletic supplier.

"Jay was always around," assistant coach Larry Bielat said. "He was almost like a member of our staff. He was a hustler as a salesman and had some great accounts. He always had deals for us.

"He'd come and tell us, 'The Detroit Lions have had an overrun of shoes and I can pick up a bunch cheap.' So George would go to Tobianski, who was in charge of the Dad's Club, and say, 'Hey, we need $2,000 to buy shoes.' And Tobianski would say, 'You've got it.' The next thing you know Louwers would pull up at the back of the school with a van full of shoes. It was always the best stuff — the best shoulder pads, the best helmets. We were the best-looking football team in the city."

Off the field as well as on. Perles implemented a dress code and bought maroon team blazers with the St. Ambrose logo on the pocket. Thank you, Dad's Club. The Cavaliers looked sharp at Sunday Mass, sitting together in the front of the church for all a proud parish to see.

St. Ambrose also was becoming a more religious team under Perles, who would troop his players over to the hall to say a rosary before games. For the big games, the team attended Mass before loading up the bus.

Like the 1962 Goodfellow Game.

"That was one of the most memorable nights in my life," said Bielat, who would go on to coach at Colorado, Michigan State, and Pitt in college. "The team dressed in the locker room in their game uniforms, then we walked across the street to Mass. They didn't have their shoes on, just the socks. It was only us and the cheerleaders in the church. We took up just the first six rows and Father Van Antwerp said Mass for us.

"Everyone went to communion and as we got up to leave, all the nuns were sitting in the back. The busses were parked right out front. As we left the church, the nuns formed a little tunnel for us to walk through. As we walked out, they gave each one of the boys a hug. None of them would go to the game. None of them could go to the game. Their order wouldn't allow it.

"But they were waiting for us after the game. As we got off the bus, the nuns were in a big circle. They must have been drinking wine as they were listening to the game. You could smell it on their breath as they were hugging us. I look at George and he looks at me and we say, 'These gals are drunk.'"

But the championship glow wore off quickly. The Cavaliers toppled Redford St. Mary, 18-13, in the 1963 season opener to extend their winning streak to 19 games. But Holy Redeemer fought St. Ambrose to a 14-14 tie. It was the first time in Greg Bringard's three-year career that his Cavaliers lined up for a football game and did not win.

"All of a sudden we felt a crack, that we weren't invincible," Bringard said. "That whole week we felt vulnerable and then boom."

The bottom fell out. Benedictine toppled the city champions, 13-7, handing them their first loss since Oct. 4, 1960.

"I just assumed Ambrose never lost," Bringard said. "So that was a shock. The Redeemer tie lingered and we fell apart against Benedictine."

Perles could not replace that great 1962 class of seniors overnight and his team collapsed, finishing 2-3-2, St. Ambrose's first non-winning season since 1955.

"That was an ugly year," Bringard said.

There were cracks in the St. Ambrose machine that were showing up off the field as well. A change in school principals meant the departure of football-friendly Sister Mary Gilbert in a transfer. Sister Marie Grace was now calling the shots.

Out-of-parish tuition had risen to $100 per family, so Perles never counted any younger brothers of players in his recruiting class. The older brother was essentially paying their tuition. Perles considered all younger brothers automatics. They wouldn't count against his allotment of 24 recruits.

But that's not how the new principal saw it. Mike Goff had two younger sisters at St. Ambrose and twin brothers on the way. He stopped by St. Ambrose on a weekend home from the University of Buffalo and Perles asked him for a favor.

"Run upstairs and talk to the principal," Perles said. "Sister Mary Gilbert said if you're family, you're in. That gave me 24 more players to recruit. But the new principal isn't buying that."

So Goff went upstairs to plead an alum's case.

"She said that's the way they did it then," Goff recalled. "But this is the way we do things now. He's allowed 24 players, and your brothers aren't part of the 24."

So the two youngest Goffs went to Servite.

Greg Hacias arrived on campus in 1963 and spent the season watching senior Joe Spada play quarterback. Like Manny Lamprides, he became a starter as a sophomore and his talent was evident. The St. Ambrose fortunes were about to turn.

Perles didn't like losing. Neither did the parish. So he put the pedal to the metal in the summer of 1964. At whatever the cost, this team was going to start winning again. So he resorted to an old Boisture trick — the illegal scrimmage.

By 1964, the two snub-nosed maroon school busses were gone, replaced by a conventional yellow school bus. When the players asked John Tobianski why he decided to scrap the maroon and whites for a yellow, the janitor said, "You don't pay sales tax on a yellow bus."

The players arrived at school one day in August and the name "ST. AMBROSE" had been taped over on the bus.

"When we were suiting up," Bringard said, "Perles told us to turn our jerseys inside out. We didn't know what was happening. So we got on the expressway and started traveling. We kept going...then all of a sudden we were crossing the Bluewater Bridge into Canada. We went to some farm and we wound up scrimmaging Austin. We didn't like Austin, so we thought it was great. We scrimmaged them in a pasture with horses and cows."

Old-time football was back. So was old-time winning.

The Cavaliers mowed down Divine Child, Redford St. Mary, Holy Redeemer, Benedictine, St. Anthony, and Servite for a 6-0 start. Next up was 4-1-1 Shrine with one of the most heralded players in the city, end Jim Seymour. He would go on to become an All-America at Notre Dame and a first-round NFL draft pick.

But Seymour and the Knights were no match for the Cavaliers, who prevailed 40-19, to finish the regular season 7-0.

"Everyone respected St. Ambrose," said Shrine's Al Fracassa, who would coach into the next century and become the winningest football coach in Michigan high school history. "We all wanted to have the same type of program. It was a very disciplined, very successful."

When the team returned to school that night, parish pastor Fr. Francis Van Antwerp told Perles and his assistants Joe Carruthers and Joe Salesky that he needed to see them in the rectory.

"We're thinking, 'Which one of us screwed up?'" Carruthers recalled. "So we go over there and sat down at a table in his office. He says, 'Boys, you did a nice job this year,' then pulled out a bottle of Schenley's OFC whiskey. He poured out four shots and said, 'Here's to you guys,' and BAM, we knocked them down. I said, 'Father, that Schenley's OFC is really unusual.' And he said, 'Yeah, boys, it's Only For Catholics.'"

Shrine may not have been a match for St. Ambrose but Detroit Cathedral was in the Soup Bowl. The Wildcats were led by all-city running back Regis Cavender, who was on his way to Michigan State. Cavender would score the Spartan touchdown in the 10-10 tie with Notre Dame in 1966.

St. Ambrose had no answer for Cavender in the first half as the Wildcats controlled the ball, the Cavaliers and the game. Cathedral led, 13-7.

"We normally ran a 5-2 defense," Bringard said. "But for some reason George went to a 6-man front in the Soup Bowl with me in the middle. They were literally killing us around the ends. I don't know why he went to a 6-1."

During a timeout late in the half, Bringard, in his capacity as a team captain, visited the sideline to confer with the coaches.

"George asked me, 'You got any suggestions?'" Bringard said. "I was kind of shocked by it. I didn't say anything."

George Perles' famous forearm drill, 1962

Photo by Fred A. Plofchan, Detroit Free Press

But Bringard thought about it on the field in the closing minute. As the team trotted to the locker room at halftime, he did offer up a suggestion to his head coach.

"Why don't you spread it out — move your tackles and your guards to the outside shoulders and just open up the middle," Bringard said. "I'll try to hold up as best I can in there. So we did that."

But the Cavaliers were about to get blistered — and not by Cathedral. Perles and the coaches talked briefly in the locker room about the defensive adjustments, then John Tobianski asked if he could have a word with the players. He also asked the coaches to leave the room.

"Tobianski literally went berserk," Bringard said. "He started hitting people. He started screaming and yelling. He was pounding people. We all started putting our helmets back on. He went ballistic. When we hit the door, we were running out of that locker room for our lives."

Led by offensive tackle Sam Bouhanna.

"He was so psyched up he ran into the door and just about knocked the damn thing off the hinges," freshman running back Tom Bialk recalled. "He didn't even open it. He tried to run right through it. That's how psyched up he was."

Playing wider defensive gaps, St. Ambrose shut out Cathedral the rest of the way. Perles also had a surprise for the Wildcats defense. Like Boisture's 132 special, Perles added a play to the game plan that week — a "transcontinental" pass from halfback Barry Boyd to spindly-legged quarterback Greg Hacias.

"We practiced the play a few times but never thought we'd need it," Hacias said. "We expected to win without throwing the ball much. I only threw 27 passes all year. Throwing the ball wasn't us."

Trailing 13-7 at the start of the fourth quarter and with the Cavaliers on their own 34, Hacias handed the ball to Boyd on an apparent sweep of right end. The quarterback continued his routine bootleg fake to the left. Around end he went, picking up speed and drifting deeper and deeper down the sideline. Hacias was 6-1, 165 pounds and wore high top black cleats like Johnny Unitas. Cathedral didn't bother with him after the handoff.

But Boyd stopped and fired the ball across the field to Hacias, who caught it at the 40. The race was on.

"Hacias wasn't a speedster and had a body like Olive Oyl," said end Tony Carducci. "There were no muscles in his body. So you were biting your nails watching that chase."

The Wildcats finally hauled Hacias down at their own 12, tackling him out of bounds. It was the only pass completion of the night for the Cavaliers. Boyd followed that up with a five-yard touchdown run and Tom Landau added a 78-yard scoring jaunt, lifting the Cavaliers to a 21-13 victory. Detroit's two best Catholic teams walked off the field with profound respect for each other, knowing that the Soup Bowl — not the Goodfellow — was the true city championship game.

"You looked up to excellence, you looked up to success," said Cavender, who would go on to become Al Fracassa's boss in the 2000s as the athletic director of Catholic League power Brother Rice.

The popularity of St. Ambrose was at its apex. For the first time ever, the Goodfellow Game would be broadcast on local television. The Cavaliers had long dressed like the Detroit Lions. Now they were commanding the same media attention as the Lions with the presence of TV cameras.

St. Ambrose wasn't concerned about PSL champion South-eastern. The Cavaliers knew they could beat the Jungaleers. Their concern that night was the snow, which held the crowd down to 15,105.

"We kept the backups in the locker room and took the first-stringers out for warm-ups," Perles said. "When we came back in, I had the backups take off their shoes and give them to the starters so they'd have dry shoes to start the game off."

With several inches of snow on the ground, the game was over before it started.

"Southeastern had a lot of speed, and the snow basically nulli-fied that," Carducci said. "They didn't have a power game. We did. So a foot of snow was perfect for us. It was wham right and wham left with a trap or counter mixed in every once in a while. All Ha-cias ever did that year was hand the ball off."

Another shutout, another Goodfellow victory, another city and state championship, this time by a 20-0 score. Landau rushed for 186 yards and all three of the game's touchdowns on 19 carries.

On Monday after the game, Perles got a call from Verdonckt's Bakery on Jefferson. It was as much a fixture in the East side neigh-borhood as Tobianski and the church. To celebrate the latest cham-pionship, the shop's Belgian proprietors wanted to prepare a spe-cial luncheon for the coaching staff. So the St. Ambrose football brain trust strolled over to Verdonckt's at noon and sat down to a Belgian delicacy — blood sausage, which consisted of sausage, duck blood and meal.

"I could hardly get it down after they told me what it was," Carruthers said. "The same with George. That first sausage kept going down and coming back, going down and coming back. It was horrible. I coughed and threw up my hand and put the sausage in my pocket. We were talking and slowly but surely we worked all of the sausages into our pockets.

"When we got up to leave they commented on how much we must have liked the sausages because we had cleaned our plates. We didn't want to embarrass them or us so we walked out of there with our pockets full of sausages. I had them in my suit pocket, in my pants pockets and headed off to school."

Bringard, a starting offensive guard whose weight dipped to 158 pounds during two-a-days in August, was named all-state in November and All-America in December. He would accept a scholarship offer from the University of Dayton — and George Perles would head off to Ohio with him.

Like Boisture, Perles had won two city titles in three years and was ready for the next challenge. The Godfather in East Lansing was still shuffling the pieces on his Midwest chessboard. Duffy Daugherty dispatched another of his Michigan State assistants, John McVay, to Dayton to become the head coach and decided Perles should join him as an assistant.

But there was no behind-the-scenes drama in the hiring of the next St. Ambrose coach. On the recommendation of Perles in his exit interview, the school promoted Carruthers, who had been his top assistant.

CLASS B

There was a price for St. Ambrose to pay for winning those state Class B football championships.

To make the jump from Class C to Class B in 1961, St. Ambrose needed an enrollment of 500-plus students and the Dad's Club needed to bankroll a minimum of four varsity sports. Enrollment increased with the success of the football program to a point that the school building on Hampton could no longer accommodate the 12 grades of students.

So St. Ambrose started bussing some of its grade schoolers into Detroit's inner city to St. Edward's on Crane. So every morning the fourth, fifth, and sixth graders would board rented city busses on Hampton for that four-mile drive west to the edge of Indian Village. That would open up classroom space at St. Ambrose for the burgeoning high-school population.

But the enrollment would remain heavily female, with never more than 175 boys in the high school at any time in the 1960s. The school's largest graduating class of the decade would be the 96 in 1963. Only 44 were boys.

That afforded all Ambrosian males the chance to earn varsity letters. The Joe D'Angelos, Bill Fourniers, Pete Genords, and Mike Goffs who chose St. Ambrose because they wanted to play multiple sports would have ample opportunity.

In addition to football, St. Ambrose fielded teams in baseball, basketball, track and, for a brief stretch from 1958-61, hockey. Tom

Beer would letter in all five sports, becoming the only Ambrosian ever to play both hockey and basketball the same winter.

"Tom [Boisture] was our basketball coach, so the practices were kind of loose," Beer said. "I'd go home after practice and eat, then get a ride to hockey practice at St. Jean. If the ice was good, we'd skate right out onto the canals."

The canal ran parallel to Alter Road for several blocks south of Jefferson, emptying into the mouth of Lake St. Clair. Many an east sider learned to play hockey on those canals in the 1950s and 1960s. When it wasn't cold enough to skate outside, a bandbox hockey rink called the "Ice Flair" on Alter and Charlevoix was available. The Cavaliers also skated at outdoor city rinks on St. Jean and at Chandler Park.

St. Ambrose needed Beer more than the basketball team did — he was the starting goalie. But the Dad's Club wasn't spending on hockey like it was football. Basketball and baseball, yes. Hockey, no. Too expensive, even for the deep pockets of the Dad's Club.

"I didn't have any goalie equipment," Beer said. "Thank God Fr. Weisner did. He also had a right-handed catching glove. So I used his goalie stuff all season. We weren't bad. We played some stiff competition."

The Cavaliers could compete with the smaller schools like Shrine and St. Alphonsus, but were no match for the larger, more organized programs at Catholic Central and Cranbrook.

The basketball team was a different story. St. Ambrose played on the court like it did on the football field — physical. Ross MacDonald, the captain of the Cooley team in that 1959 Goodfellow Game, played football at Michigan State. Ironically, his roommate was Larry Bringard, the 1958 All-America from St. Ambrose. MacDonald recalls pickup basketball games with Bringard and some of his buddies.

"They played commando basketball," MacDonald said. "There was no finesse in the way they played. You'd get killed out there."

But not on the scoreboard. Every team in Michigan participated in the state high-school basketball tournament. It was single elimination — one loss and you're out. During the 1960s, St. Ambrose posted a 2-10 record in state tournament play.

The Cavaliers were surrounded by basketball talent on the East side. Two neighboring schools, Detroit Austin and Grosse Pointe St. Paul, reached state title games a combined six times from 1957-69. Holy Redeemer, which competed in the same football league with St. Ambrose, won a state basketball championship in 1960. Servite also was a perennial power on the East side. St. Paul and Servite combined to end five St. Ambrose basketball seasons in tournament play in the 1960s.

But those schools recruited basketball players. St. Ambrose did not.

"I played no football until I got to St. Ambrose," Ray Federspiel said. "I wasn't enthused about playing football. Basketball is what I wanted to play. But Boisture said if you don't play football, you don't play basketball. So I had no other option but to play football."

The Class of 1963 that included Beer, Goff, Cory Richardson, Ron Albers, and Pete Piazza provided the most competitive basketball team of the decade for St. Ambrose. Those 1963 Cavaliers were one of only two teams to win a state tournament game in the 1960s. They competed on sheer athleticism.

Four days after winning the 1962 Goodfellow Game against Cooley, the Cavaliers trotted onto the court to play Holy Redeemer. The Lions were to basketball what the Cavaliers were to football in the Catholic Double-A.

"With one practice under our belt, we're beating them at the end of three quarters," St. Ambrose basketball coach Larry Bielat said. "I couldn't believe it. We were playing with the same great intensity that we played football. We had them on the ropes — then our legs gave out on us. Those poor kids had nothing left for the fourth quarter and Holy Redeemer came back and beat us."

St. Ambrose basketball, 1962

Photo courtesy Tom Beer

After winning the City Championship, football players Tom Beer (35) and Cory Richardson (40) played their first varsity basketball game.
Photo by Jerry Heiman, Detroit Free Press

When St. Ambrose was not able to compete against Holy Redeemer, the Cavaliers found ways of balancing the court against the Lions.

"We couldn't beat them if God was on our side," said Joe Carruthers, who would succeed Bielat as the basketball coach. "We had football players playing basketball. So we're playing Holy Redeemer home one night at Servite. The basketball is always supplied by the home team. So I let the air out a little and we practiced with it all week. When it came time to play the game, the ref asked the Holy Redeemer coach [Joe Lascola] if he wanted to check the ball. He waved him off and said, 'No, let's get started. Let's go.'

"We had about a five-point lead on them at half. Every time they tried to bounce the ball it wouldn't come back up. They kept turning the ball over in the first half and Joe was going crazy. They wound up beating us by one and went on to win the Catholic League championship that year. He said afterwards, 'I learned something from a football coach.'"

The Cavaliers had basketball talent. The likes of Mike Cure, Tom Beer, Gary Nowak, and Paul Hayner could compete on the hardwood with the city's best players. Nowak would play in a Detroit summer league in the mid-1960s on a team with former University of Michigan standouts Cazzie Russell and Oliver Darden, and the Wolverines would offer Nowak a basketball scholarship. But the teamwork and drive that existed in football at St. Ambrose did not carry over to the basketball court.

"We were terrible," Nowak said.

Baseball was even worse. The team played its home games on the backside of Belle Isle, almost as if to be hidden from sight.

"If we ever won a game," Nowak said, "it was a fluke."

But baseball was a respite for the St. Ambrose football players. The Cavaliers didn't have enough manpower to field both a baseball and a track team, so on days St. Ambrose was scheduled to play both a baseball game and a track meet, the coaches had to make a decision. There was only one team bus.

"If they were in a good mood," Nowak said, "they'd let us play baseball and call and forfeit the track meet. If they were in a bad mood, they'd force the football team to get on the bus and go to the track meet and we'd forfeit the baseball game."

The Cavaliers were far more competitive in track than they were in either baseball or basketball because of all the football speed Boisture and Perles recruited. In 1960, the St. Ambrose relay team of D'Angelo, Fournier, Lantzy, and freshman Mike Goff won the Catholic League title and qualified for the state meet. They earned all-state honors by placing at that meet.

Pete Genord experienced one of his most lasting athletic thrills on a high-school track. The Detroit public and parochial schools staged a rare city meet on the same day at the same track. Some events mixed the public and parochial school teams and Genord was running the anchor leg for St. Ambrose in one such relay event.

"I had the opportunity to run against Henry Carr," Genord said. "We were running in the 880 in a heat with Northwestern. I had a 30-yard lead when I got the baton. By the time I came out of the turn Carr had passed me by 20 yards."

Carr went on to set a world record in the 200 meters. He won an NCAA title at Arizona State in 1963 and an Olympic gold medal in 1964.

The St. Ambrose track experience was slapstick at times because of the long-standing rule implemented by Boisture that the football players must participate in a spring sport. Baseball was a game of skill, and many of the football players either lacked that skill or the desire to play the sport. That left track.

"If you were a back or wide receiver, you'd run the sprints," said end Tony Carducci, who was recruited in 1963. "Everyone else had to run the mile. So at track meets they'd have a first call for the mile and St. Ambrose would send out 30 guys — all of our linemen.

"Everybody would come up to the line in these thin, paper-weight shoes — and our guys would have their high-top football shoes on. The real milers would run a 4:30 and then have to wait for all of our big fat linemen to finish the race in 8-9 minutes."

When the St. Ambrose 880-relay team placed in the state track meet in 1960, that gave Goff a rare red stripe on his letter sweater as a freshman.

After an Ambrosian lettered in his first sport, he'd pay a visit to the Detroit Knitting Mills on Gratiot and Russell and order his maroon letter sweater. A white stripe was sewn in for each year you lettered, and colored stripes could be added for any honors. A yellow stripe signified all-city, a red all-state and a blue All-America. Team captains earned a star patch and each championship entitled you to a circular patch. The 1961 team, for instance, received three patches — Catholic League champions, city champions, and state champions.

Tom Beer left St. Ambrose with the most decorated letter sweater in school history. He ran out of room on his sleeves for all the stripes and patches.

Beer earned four white stripes for lettering as a freshman, sophomore, junior, and senior. He earned four yellow all-city stripes for basketball as a junior and senior plus football and baseball as a senior. He earned a red all-state and blue All-America stripe for football as a senior.

"I didn't put a stripe on for all-city baseball my senior year," Beer said. "To be honest, I was getting kind of embarrassed so I stopped putting them on."

Beer also earned a captain's star for football plus six championship patches in 1961 and 1962.

"I had three patches on one arm from the Goodfellow Games, plus city, Catholic, and state B champs, then my senior year on the other sleeve I had city champs and B champs," Beer said. "I left the Catholic off because I didn't have any room. It's in a suitcase somewhere."

Football was always the feature attraction for grade school recruits of St. Ambrose. But baseball continued to be a perk.

DEAN OF MEN

Joe Carruthers was more than the new football coach at St. Ambrose. Like George Perles and Tom Boisture before him, he was the school's Dean of Men.

The Dominican nuns delivered discipline at the school but the football coaches provided the muscle.

"The football program there was so strong it dominated the whole school," Carruthers said. "That generated an easier teaching environment for the nuns. They didn't have any problems. All they had to say was, 'Coach, can you handle this?' I'd say, 'I sure can, Sister.'"

Carruthers kept a canoe paddle at his office in the coal bin as his tool for the administration of justice. Half-dollar sized holes were bored into the paddle end.

"It would whistle when you swung it," Carruthers said. "That usually kept them in line. Sometimes a good talk did the trick. You'd put the fear of God in them. Those kids were toeing the line. Plus their moms and dads were tickled to death that we were all over their fannies keeping them on the straight and narrow."

Perles gave Gary Nowak the belt once. He was the biggest kid in school, nicknamed the Jolly Green Giant. Nowak started at end on Goodfellow champions in 1964 and 1966 and would go on to play at Michigan State and in the NFL with the San Diego Chargers. He was summoned to the principal's office as an underclassman and owned up to attending a party where alcohol was served. He received his punishment right there — in front of Sr. Marie Grace.

"She was excusing herself to leave," Nowak recalled, "and George said, 'Oh no, you're not leaving.' He made her stay and watch, then gave me two whacks with the belt."

Carruthers recalled one other player getting paddled during the Perles era.

"His father came over to see George and I in the coal bin," Carruthers said. "Father Van Antwerp was there. The dad said, 'You can't do that to my kid. That ain't right.' Father Van asked him, 'Did he know the rules?' The dad, said, 'Yeah.' So Father Van said to me, 'Coach, will you go upstairs and get his records?'

"So I went upstairs and got his records, brought them back down and Father Van handed them to his father and said, 'Here's his records. Take your kid over to Denby.' The dad almost had a heart attack right there. He said, 'No, no, I don't want him to leave school. You can't do this. Everything is going to be alright, Father.' He left and that was the end of that.'"

It wasn't just the football players who were disciplined by the coaches. In the one year Larry Bielat served as an assistant under Perles in 1962, he owned a pair of shears and would give the players haircuts before the start of two-a-days.

"One day Sr. Mary Gilbert calls me down to the office and tells me, 'Take this guy here and cut his hair down. He obviously can't afford it, and I'm tired of telling him to get his hair cut,'" Bielat recalled.

So Bielat marched the student to the locker room, sat him on one of the benches and told him, "I'll be as careful as I can, young fella, but this hair is coming off."

Bielat went up one side and down the other, giving the kid a buzz cut. The student was not happy with his new look. The next day at practice, Bielat discovered there was someone else unhappy with the haircut — the boy's father, who drove to Defer, stormed onto the practice field and demanded to know which coach was Bielat.

"Are you Bielat?" the man yelled. "I hope you've got a good lawyer because I'm suing you for what you did to my son."

"Whoa," Bielat responded. "Wait a minute. Sr. Mary Gilbert told me to do that and she's my boss."

"I don't care who told you to do it," the man said. "You're not a barber and you made a mess of my kid's hair — and I'm suing you. I'll see you at school tomorrow."

The next morning Bielat visited the principal's office before class and told Sr. Mary Gilbert he had been threatened with a lawsuit.

"He's already called," the nun said. "He'll be here in a few minutes. I want you in my office when he arrives."

So the three visitors — football coach, disgruntled parent and nearly bald son — sat down with the St. Ambrose principal.

"I'm so happy to see you here," Sr. Mary Gilbert told the dad. "Do you know how many times I've called you? But you're either at work or the country club. It seems you're always too busy to come in and see me. In fact, you're too busy to get this son of a gun's haircut. So I had Coach Bielat cut his hair and he did a fine job."

"Wait a minute, Sister," the parent responded. "That was a lousy job. I've already called my lawyer and he's going to be getting hold of Coach Bielat."

"Called your lawyer?" Sr. Mary Gilbert said. "I'm happy to hear that. I'd like to meet this guy. But first off I'll tell you what — if you don't like the way I run St. Ambrose, you take that kid of yours and the both of you get the hell out of here. Go to a public school."

Bielat's eyebrows shot up in surprise at the nun's tone, choice of words and message.

"Wait a minute," the parent said. "I want him here. I graduated from here. My wife graduated from here. We live in the parish. I want my son graduating from here."

"Then start liking that haircut," the principal said, "because I love it. Now get the hell out of here."

Photo courtesy Dave Vitali

Sister Mary Gilbert

Father and son left, leaving the principal alone with Bielat.

"Don't worry about a thing," she said. "Everything is under control. We won't hear from that guy again."

And they didn't.

As the years went by, the St. Ambrose coaches would give the captains greater ownership of the team. They would make the phone calls to ensure their teammates made the nightly 9 p.m. curfew. The captains would have to dole out punishment to any offenders. That kept the hands of the coaches clean.

"Perles had me discipline them," said Greg Bringard, captain of the 1964 team. "There were only three or four. Sometimes I used the belt, other times the paddle."

When Boisture arrived in 1956, he introduced boxing gloves to the world of St. Ambrose discipline. If two players fought on the practice field, the coaches would quickly break it up and tell them they could fight later. Then after practice, the entire team would troop over to the hall to watch the two players strap on the gloves and flail away. If there were fights in the locker room or on the school grounds, the two combatants wound up in the hall with the gloves on over the lunch hour.

"George [Perles] would say, 'Boys, we can't watch films today. We have to go to the gym and watch a fight,'" Tony Carducci said. "So we'd grab our lunch bags and say, 'OK,' then get in a circle just like you would the streets of Detroit and watch the two guys go at it. They'd put on the gloves and they'd have to beat the hell out of each other. You got so tired punching the last thing you ever wanted to do was get into a fight."

Boxing also became a part of the physical education classes. Sometimes the fights would be tag-teams with the four fighters wearing one glove apiece. Sometimes the coaches would stack the boxing card with football players versus non-football players. Fair-mindedness was not always part of the equation. But boxing "class" in the Carruthers era ended forevermore when one of his star football players was knocked silly by a haymaker.

31

LAST CHAMP

Greg Hacias loved baseball. His best friend, Greg Wilczynski, was the son of the legendary high school baseball coach at Catholic League power St. Ladislaus, Frank Wilczynski. The two played ball from sun up to sun down, six months out of the year. Hacias spent the other three months in the fall playing football and three months in the winter playing basketball.

Hacias was a pitcher/shortstop in baseball and, because of his arm, a quarterback in football. But basketball and football were afterthoughts. Hacias knew he was going to follow in the footsteps of the Paciorek brothers and become a baseball star at St. Lad's.

"It was a slam dunk," he said.

His father was the manager of the Hughes, Hatcher & Suffrin men's clothing store at Seven Mile and Mack, and one day George Perles walked in.

"We hear your son's a pretty good football player," the St. Ambrose coach told Ed Hacias, "and we'd like to talk to him."

The next thing Greg Hacias knew, the St. Ambrose football coach was joining his family at the dinner table.

"My mom would make a big Polish meal," Hacias said, "and Perles would never turn down a meal. George was actually recruiting my dad — and my dad was getting really excited about the idea of me playing for St. Ambrose."

Perles invited Hacias to the 1962 Goodfellow Game. That spring he also invited him to attend a St. Ambrose baseball game at Manz Field, a handsome amateur ballpark on the East side of town. Perles also was the head baseball coach. The Cavaliers were struggling that day with Joe Spada on the mound.

So Perles put his beefy arm around the skinny shoulders of his football recruit.

"Son," Perles told Hacias, "if you come to St. Ambrose, I will promise you right here and now that you will pitch next year as a freshman on this varsity baseball team on this field."

Hacias might have to wait his turn in the talent-rich St. Ladislaus program. But Perles was willing to move him to the top of the baseball queue at St. Ambrose.

"That got my attention," Hacias said. "That sold me. Unbeknownst to me, my dad had already made the decision I was going there."

Hacias pitched as a freshman for the St. Ambrose baseball team. He also started at guard on the basketball team. But he watched from the sideline as the Cavaliers slogged through a rare losing football season in 1963. Hacias never took a snap.

But Perles installed Hacias at quarterback as a sophomore in 1964. He spent the season handing off to Barry Boyd and Tom Landau as the Cavaliers pounded out a perfect 9-0 record. Hacias threw only 27 passes that season but 10 went for touchdowns.

"Teams always had 10 men in the box against us," Hacias said. "So any passes we threw were completely unexpected."

But all that would change in 1965. The departure of Perles left Joe Carruthers in charge.

"George is a great coach who loves to run the football," Carruthers told the Cavaliers at his first team meeting. "But I kind of like the idea of passing. We're going to open this thing up."

The head coach wasn't the only change for the St. Ambrose football team in 1965. The Cavaliers were leaving Mack Park for Keyworth Stadium, a larger venue in a better part of town.

"We had a good following at Mack Park," Gary Nowak said. "We'd always fill the place. So when we first went over to Keyworth,

Photo courtesy Wayne Joseph

Greg Hacias

you wondered what kind of crowds we'd have. But we'd fill that place, too. We were drawing 11,000 people to games.

"What I found so amazing was that people with no ties to St. Ambrose would follow us. Joe Blow from wherever, who had no kids going there and no real tie to the school. But he'd come to every game. No matter where we played, the stands would be full."

But trouble was brewing in the Catholic Double-A. Dearborn Divine Child won two consecutive Catholic League Second Division titles in 1961-62. The Falcons moved up to First Division in 1963 and sent an immediate message to the champs. Divine Child thumped St. Ambrose, 27-19, in their first meeting on the way to a 5-2 record at the higher level of competition.

But Perles squared his ledger in 1964 when Boyd kicked the first field goal in school history in the final minute to defeat Divine Child, 9-7, in the opener. It was the only loss the Falcons suffered all season. Divine Child was coming — and coming fast.

But Perles left in 1965, and the Dearborn problem now belonged to Carruthers. Enrollment was dipping at St. Ambrose, slipping under 400 students. That dropped the Cavaliers back into Class C. Dearborn was booming in the 1960s, and so was Class B Divine Child. Even though St. Ambrose was the defending Catholic, city, and state champion, Divine Child was the preseason choice to win the Catholic Double A.

The showdown between the two powers came in the second week of the season at Dearborn's Edsel Ford Field. At the start of the second half, Divine Child held a 6-0 lead with St. Ambrose pinned at its own 1-yard line.

On second-and-10, Carruthers called a look-in pass to senior end Jim Heidisch. He dropped it.

"Run it again," Carruthers told junior Tony Carducci, who was alternating with Heidisch as couriers shuttling in the plays to Hacias. Carducci didn't drop it — and 99 yards later he was in the end zone. Carducci caught one other pass late in the fourth quarter for a 26-yard touchdown and the Cavaliers prevailed, 20-6.

Carruthers received a handwritten note that week from Tom Boisture, who was still at the University of Houston.

"That took balls," wrote Boisture of Carruthers' decision to pass from his own end zone.

The Cavaliers hadn't thrown the ball the entire decade, much less from their own end zone. St. Ambrose came to define the term "power football" under Perles. But under Carruthers, that era was at an end. Hacias threw and threw and threw. The Cavaliers sat 5-0, outscoring the opposition 140-32.

"We caught everyone by surprise," Hacias said. "We were St. Ambrose, a running team. But all of a sudden we go from throwing the ball three times a game [in 1964] to 27 times a game. It took 3-4 games before people figured us out. We walked through everyone that year."

Game 6 was the biggest walkover — Harper Woods Bishop Gallagher. The school opened in 1962 and 1965 would be the first season the Lancers played at the First Division level.

Homecomings in high school are festive occasions. Each class builds a float and they parade around the field at halftime, when the queen and her court are introduced. Schools generally schedule an opponent they know they can defeat for their homecoming game. Why spoil the evening with a loss?

Surprisingly, Bishop Gallagher selected St. Ambrose for its homecoming game in 1965. When their bus pulled into the stadium parking lot, the Cavaliers caught a glimpse of the floats. One had a coffin with a dummy dressed in a St. Ambrose uniform wearing No. 10 — Hacias' number. Another of the floats had a St. Ambrose dummy hanging from a noose. That dummy also wore number 10.

St. Ambrose received death threats at the school that week — if Hacias plays, he'll be gunned down. There were discussions between the school and the Hacias family.

"My dad says, 'He's playing,'" Hacias recalled. "So did I."

Hacias threw four touchdown passes and St. Ambrose set a school record for points, blasting Bishop Gallagher 59-6. The Cavaliers finished up a 7-0 regular season with a 27-7 triumph over Servite, earning a fourth trip to a Soup Bowl in seven years. It also would be the second time in four years St. Ambrose would square off with Harper Woods Notre Dame for the Catholic League title.

St. Ambrose was now recruiting heavily in the St. Clair Shores area and several of its best players were swiped from traditional Notre Dame neighborhoods. Carducci went to St. Ambrose even though his older brother had gone to Notre Dame. The Irish were very familiar rivals.

"We knew all the guys on the East side," Carducci said. "Everyone I knew went to either Austin or Notre Dame. Everybody on our team knew somebody from Notre Dame. My best friend went to Notre Dame. So when we played those games it was always a backyard war."

That war raged the entire evening between two evenly matched teams until Hacias hit Carducci with a 12-yard, fourth-down touchdown pass in the fourth quarter to put St. Ambrose on top. When the clock ticked down to 70 seconds with the Cavaliers clinging to a 21-20 lead, another Catholic League championship was in the bag....Or so Carruthers thought when he spoke into the headset to his assistant coach Joe D'Angelo upstairs in the coaching booth.

"C'mon down," Carruthers told him. "It's over."

But it wasn't. Dave Baldyga returned a St. Ambrose punt 77 yards in the final minute to deliver Notre Dame an electrifying 27-21 victory. The Irish would be headed for the Goodfellow Game, not the Cavaliers.

"That was the worst feeling of my life," Carruthers said.

Football season was over for the 1965 Cavaliers. But it was the shortest offseason in school history.

"It was traumatic," Carducci said. "We were in the bus crying after the game. We couldn't believe we lost. Then it turned into hate. We started the very next day working towards Notre Dame. Our whole focus became playing Notre Dame again in the next Soup Bowl."

There was one consolation prize — Hacias was selected as the all-state quarterback. He threw 15 touchdown passes that season and rushed for three more scores.

"He worked as hard as anyone on that team," Carruthers said. "He was one of those unique kids you get once in your lifetime."

St. Ambrose would give Hacias some help in 1966 with the return of an old friend — the running game.

In 1965, the Cavaliers shuffled four backs into the offense, juniors Martinelli and Rich Bommarito and sophomores Tom Bialk and Bob Walker. The upper classmen allowed the Cavaliers to be good, but Bialk and Walker would give the Cavaliers potential for greatness. Bialk was a compact, physical power runner. Walker, well, St. Ambrose had never seen a back quite like him before.

"He was a freak of nature," Carducci said. "He was 6-3, 220 and could outsprint everyone. No one beat our 880-relay team with me, Bialk, Heidisch, and Walker. Everyone would hold their own and then we'd give the baton to Walker. He'd blow anyone away."

One of the best passing attacks in the city returned intact in 1966 with Hacias, Carducci, and tight end Gary Nowak. Now it would be paired with one of the city's best rushing attacks in Bialk and Walker. The swagger was back.

But swagger took a thumping in the season opener against Servite. On a suffocating hot day at Mack Park, the Panthers unleashed a new quarterback, sophomore Frank Kolch, and a new offense on the Cavaliers.

"They threw the ball all over the field," recalled Nowak, who played defensive rover that day. "We'd never seen anything like it. I don't think they ran the ball twice the whole game. He'd throw it five, 10, 30 yards…it didn't matter. It seemed like they had 7-8 guys in every pass pattern. It was a hot day and we were going nuts. But we got through it."

Barely. Kolch threw for 344 yards, including touchdown bombs of 87, 82, and 40 yards. But the Cavaliers prevailed, 34-26, on the strength of Bialk's three second-half touchdowns. St. Ambrose shut out Shrine (19-0), thumped Divine Child (32-14), and matched its 7-0 regular season record of 1965.

Yes, Notre Dame would be awaiting St. Ambrose in the Soup Bowl again. And this version of the Fighting Irish appeared to be even better than the 1965 team that shared the city championship by tying Denby, 14-14, in the Goodfellow Game. The 1966 Irish

1966 game vs. Denby: #16 Tom Bialk (with the ball), #10 Greg Hacias

Photo by Jerry Heiman, Detroit Free Press, courtesy Wayne Joseph

rolled up 274 points in the regular season, slapping 60 points on DeLaSalle, 53 apiece on both Brother Rice and Cathedral, and 49 on Salesian.

The explosive Notre Dame offense wasn't the foremost concern of Carruthers; the explosive element of his own offense was. Carducci was struggling physically. He needed to have fluid drained from his knee before every game. Team physician Dr. Robert Gerow would extract the fluid with "a ten-penny needle," Carducci recalled. "It was excruciating. I couldn't move until the game. Then after the game it would fill up again."

Carducci may have been the toughest player on the Cavaliers. He broke his nose five times in his high-school career, including four on the practice field. But the extraction of fluid from his knee was becoming more painful by the week. By the end of the season, Carruthers, trainer John Tobianski, and the biggest Cavalier Gary Nowak were holding Carducci down when the needle was plunged.

Carducci should not have played in the Soup Bowl. But he had been training all year for this one game. The broken noses and the seven fluid extractions were just part of the price he was willing to pay for another crack at Notre Dame.

So Carducci went under the needle an eighth time in 1966 on the evening of the Soup Bowl, having the blood and fluid extracted from his swollen knee.

"You could see the tears coming out of his eyes," Carruthers said. "I'm thinking, 'I can't play him.' John said, 'He'll be alright.' John taped him up, helped him off the table and told him to go lay down for a while. I saw tears coming out of John's eyes. We were all crying.

"He played and had a fantastic night. That's the kind of kids we had at St. Ambrose. He was unbelievable."

The Cavaliers couldn't have beaten Notre Dame that night without Carducci. For that matter, the Cavaliers couldn't have beaten Notre Dame that night without Carducci's brother John. Five years older than Tony, John was a Notre Dame alum and knew the Irish as well he knew his brother's Cavaliers. John gave Tony a scouting report on Notre Dame quarterback Rick Wenner: "He carries the ball like a loaf of bread. You can steal it from him."

And Carducci did steal it with six minutes remaining in the fourth quarter of a scoreless game, crashing in from his linebacker spot on a rollout and wrenching the ball from Wenner's grasp. The turnover came at midfield and paved the way for the game's only touchdown on a one-yard run by Rich Bommarito.

But the contest again surged to the final seconds with Notre Dame on the verge of another heart-stopping victory. Baldyga delivered the dagger in the 1965 Soup Bowl and appeared poised to deliver again.

Baldyga wheeled out of the backfield down the far sideline, seemingly unnoticed by the St. Ambrose defenders. Wenner fired a cross-field pass to Baldyga, who raced 52 yards with it. But 145-pound defensive back Bob Bott dove at his ankles, tripping him up inside the St. Ambrose 5 as time expired. Game over — St. Ambrose held the most explosive offensive Catholic team in the city scoreless on the way to a 6-0 victory.

Carruthers met with a gaggle of press covering the game afterward. *Detroit News* columnist Pete Waldmeier asked the St. Ambrose coach if there was a sense of déjà vu when he saw Baldyga heading for the end zone in the final minute of a Soup Bowl for the second consecutive year.

"That Notre Dame kid was running for a touchdown," Carruthers cracked, "but Bobby Bott was running for his life."

Bott's tackle would send St. Ambrose to its fifth city championship game in eight years. It would be the first time the Cavaliers played East side rival Denby — but the third time they would see Roger Parmentier. He left Cooley for Denby in 1964 and his son Gary was now his star running back.

The 1966 Tars were the most talented team Parmentier had ever taken to a Goodfellow Game. They were the highest scoring team in the city with 333 points. Denby paddled Southeastern 42-0 for the PSL championship and ran up 62 points on Kettering, 54 on Osborn and 53 on Northeastern. The Tars shut out half of their eight opponents and allowed only 40 points all season.

But for the first time in the 29-year history of the Goodfellow Game, the city championship would not be played at Tiger Stadium. The NFL implemented a rule that year that prohibited another game from being played on one of its fields within 48 hours of an NFL game. The Lions were scheduled to play the Baltimore Colts at home that Sunday, so the Goodfellow Game needed to find a new home.

The city championship was moved to the University of Detroit, where the No. 2 team in Class A (Denby) would meet the No. 2 team in Class C (St. Ambrose). But there was a bigger game being played later that day in East Lansing — No. 1 Michigan State

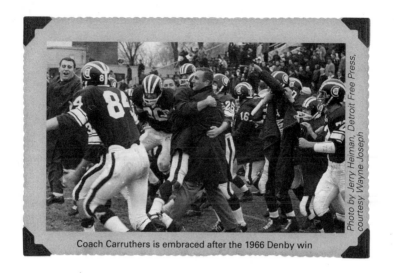

Coach Carruthers is embraced after the 1966 Denby win

Photo by Jerry Heiman, Detroit Free Press, courtesy Wayne Joseph

versus No. 2 Notre Dame. To accommodate interest in that "Game of the Century," kickoff for the Goodfellow Game was moved up to a 10:30 a.m. As a result, only 12,337 turned out.

"We never drank beer during the season," Carducci said. "But when we pulled up that day for the Goodfellow Game, you could hear the bottles rattling in the trunk. We were going to win the championship, then we were going to party."

And party they did. Denby would score on St. Ambrose — the first public-school team to reach the end zone against the Cavaliers since Parmentier's Cooley Cardinals in 1959. But Tom Bialk rushed for two touchdowns and Carducci returned a Denby fumble nine yards for another score, powering the Cavaliers to a 33-19 victory.

Roger Parmentier is in the Michigan High School Football Coaches Hall of Fame with more than 100 career victories. But he was 0-3 against St. Ambrose, with each loss spoiling a perfect season and costing him a state championship.

"I scrimmaged everybody: Riverview, South Lake, Lake Shore, DeLaSalle, Hazel Park," Parmentier said. "I called all the good teams to get our kids used to playing that caliber of opponent. It seemed like we'd murder those teams. Then we'd get to St. Ambrose...they were just better than we were."

That amazed Carruthers.

"At the end of the season we were beating the Class A teams," Carruthers said. "If they saw us in the shower room, they'd have beaten the living daylights out of us. We had a bunch of skinny little kids — Hacias, Bott, (Ron) Biotti, (Doug) Martinelli.... It was amazing the ability of those kids to surpass mentally."

32

LAST HURRAH

Tom Bialk was the Paul Hornung of the 1966 state champion St. Ambrose Cavaliers.

Hornung was listed as a halfback for the Green Bay Packers in the 1960s but played the game beyond his job description. He ran, passed, caught, and kicked the football on his way to the Pro Football Hall of Fame.

Bialk kicked off for the Cavaliers in 1966. In the Divine Child game he threw a 74-yard touchdown pass to Gary Nowak and caught a 20-yarder from Greg Hacias. He returned punts and kick-offs and would launch an occasional quick kick to dig the Cavaliers out of a hole. Bialk also was the only running back from either the Detroit Catholic or city league to earn all-state honors in 1966 from the Associated Press. He rushed for 14 touchdowns as a junior that season and passed for two more.

"He was really something," Joe Carruthers said. "He scored almost every touchdown for us. He did it all — and boy was he tough. If you were in a foxhole, you'd definitely want him in there with you."

The Cavaliers found out how mentally tough Bialk was in the 1966 Soup Bowl and how physically tough he was in the Goodfellow Game.

Coming off the field after a hard-fought 6-0 victory over Notre Dame in the Soup Bowl, his uniform scarred with grass and dirt from countless trips to the turf, Carruthers grabbed Bialk by the shoulder pad, stuck out his hand and said, "Great game."

Tom Bialk

Bialk accepted the congratulations with the knowledge that he did have a great game — blocking. Even though he was the best runner in the city, the Cavaliers decided to feature the bigger Bob Walker against Notre Dame.

"Bobby ran wild that night," Bialk said.

Bialk was O.K. with that game plan. He and fellow running backs Walker, Rich Bommarito, Doug Martinelli, and Alex Joseph made a pact before the start of the season.

"If you carried the ball, the other guys would block," Bialk said. "It was all luck of the draw. Whatever the coaches called, we did. There wasn't any single-mindedness. It was all very unselfish."

They all knew the next week could be a different story for any of them. In Bialk's case, it would be a different story.

"We're going to cut you loose in the Goodfellow Game," Carruthers promised Bialk as the two walked off the field after the Soup Bowl.

Denby won the coin toss and elected to receive in the city championship game. Bialk was on the kickoff team and made a beeline toward Bruce Webb as the Denby back charged up the middle of the field with the football.

"In the old days you were trained to stick your face in there," Bialk said. "So I stuck my face in there…and got knocked out."

Trainer John Tobianski trotted out with the smelling salts and the Cavaliers had Bialk back on his feet in no time. But Carruthers held him out of the game's first two series as the cobwebs cleared. When Bialk hit the field again, he arrived with a vengeance. He rushed for 85 yards and two touchdowns on 14 carries in that 33-19 rout of Denby.

But Bialk was diagnosed with a sprained neck and spent the night in a hospital. He spent the next month sleeping on the hardwood floor in the front room of his house because of the pain.

"It was a great win," Bialk said, "but I didn't get the chance to enjoy it until three or four months later when the pain was gone."

In the 1967 season opener against Bishop Gallagher, Bialk was bounced out of bounds on a sweep and landed in his head. Again he was knocked silly and again X-rays were taken.

"They discovered I had three cracked vertebra in my neck," Bialk said. "It turns out I played the whole Goodfellow Game with a broken neck. I could have been a quadriplegic. To this day I thank God and whoever else was involved for not sustaining anything more serious."

Mickey Carter found out how tough Bialk was that winter when the football team staged its annual boxing card in the hall. Carruthers would pair off the entire roster for an afternoon of boxing. The matches would be posted in the locker room a few days early to give everyone the chance to develop a healthy case of angst.

"There are certain things that scared you in life that always remain with you," said Paul Hayner, a sophomore on that 1967 team. "That was one of them. You were so nervous leading up to it you couldn't eat."

Perles implemented the boxing card during his tenure as coach and Carruthers continued the tradition. The coaches would toss a foam rubber wrestling mat on the floor and the football team would surround the square, forming pseudo ropes for a boxing ring. Then the coaches would strap the 16-ounce gloves and head gear on the two combatants. Carruthers would blow his whistle to start the match and, after he had seen enough, blow his whistle again to bring the fight to its conclusion. Sometimes the match would last three minutes, sometimes 10 — however long it took both kids to punch themselves out.

"If a coach wanted to see someone get his ass kicked, they'd set it up," Hayner said. "The mats made no sense. Most of the hitting was done off the mats. You'd see guys get thrown into the radiators. It was encouraged by the upper classmen. I don't know if you could even call it boxing. They just wanted to see you go berserk."

"There were no rules," Carter added. "If you knocked a guy down you'd jump on him. I remember in one of my fights I threw a guy into the Coke machine and a lot of the bottles broke. You'd see guys get their faces rearranged. It was hellacious."

Bialk remembered one match when he was an underclassman between Norbert Skorupski — dubbed "Nasty Nibby" by his teammates — and Jerry Nantais.

"There were these swinging doors at one end of the gym," Bialk said. "They went flying out those doors punching each other, then came flying back in. It was like a barroom brawl.

"Guys were just kicking ass. The coaches wanted to see how tough you were. It was vicious, mean stuff. Guys were getting hurt. You were fighting for your life."

At the other end of the gym was an elevated stage, and at the back of the stage were two sinks.

"When you were done fighting, you'd go up there and throw up," Bialk said. "It was that tough."

Bialk anticipated a session with the sink in the spring of 1967 when he learned Carruthers had paired him off with Carter, a defensive lineman. At 5-9, 170 pounds, Bialk would normally be fighting a few weight classes lower than the 6-0, 195-pound Carter. The match mystified Carter.

"I thought, 'Why the heck am I fighting Bialk?'" Carter said. "The seniors usually fought the juniors to toughen them up a little bit. When I was a junior I fought [senior Tony] Piccione and held my own. I was strong, but Bialk was probably the toughest kid in our class. I guess Carruthers wanted to teach the other guys about fighting."

But it didn't mystify Bialk. He remembers driving to downtown Detroit for the all-state banquet in December 1966 with his coach.

"Don't think for a minute there aren't 100 other guys who could be sitting in your place," Carruthers said. "It's all politics."

That was the St. Ambrose way — build your stars up, then knock them down. Tom Boisture did it to Joe D'Angelo, George Perles did it to Mike Van Goethem, and now Carruthers was doing it with Bialk.

"He kept my head small," Bialk said. "I probably needed it back then."

The boxing match with the rough-and-tumble Carter was another message to Bialk: that red stripe on your letter sweater doesn't make you better than anyone else on this football team.

"I think the coaches wanted to see me get my ass kicked," Bialk said.

But it wasn't to be. When Carruthers blew the whistle the two combatants raced at each other and Bialk landed the first punch flush to Carter's face, breaking his nose.

"He couldn't see a thing and I was able to finish him off," Bialk said. "To this day I tell him I got lucky. If he could see me I'm sure he would have cleaned my clock. I thought I was going to catch mine that day."

This wasn't what Hayner envisioned when he enrolled at St. Ambrose in 1966. He expected to follow his older brother Glen to Servite and play basketball as well as football. Under Jack Carroll, Servite had reached the Class B regional basketball finals in both 1964 and 1965.

"Basketball was my first love," Hayner said. "I was all set to go to Servite. I was looking forward to playing for Jack. But Mike [football coach D'Angelo] told us St. John Berchmans had such a large eighth-grade class that year that the football team wasn't going to be allowed to bring in any outsiders. Mike said they couldn't pull any strings."

So Hayner went to St. Ambrose, where he became a three-year starter in football and a four-year starter in basketball. The importance of football was driven home to him in spring of 1968 on a day the Cavaliers were scheduled to play their opening-round state tournament basketball game against Grosse Pointe St. Paul.

"Here we are, going to play a state power," Hayner recalled, "and they scheduled the boxing matches that same day. I'm hours away from having to guard some of the best players in the city — and I've got the boxing gloves on.

"But how you fared in your match had a big say in your position on the football team the next fall. I got my guy in a headlock and was hitting him as hard as I could. I went crazy. All I remember is being dead tired afterwards."

That night St. Paul's basketball players whipped St. Ambrose's football players, 57-43.

Hayner would go on to play football at Michigan State and then spend 30-plus years teaching in the Detroit public school system. Decades later, he shakes his head at the memory of those boxing matches.

"I've been in charge of kids all my life," Hayner said. "If something like that ever happened now, there'd be lawsuits everywhere. But if you went to St. Ambrose and played football, this was all part of being a champion. Everything was geared to man-on-man competition. How are you going to react? Are you going to compete? They wanted to see what you had inside."

The Class of 1968 had never lost a regular-season game. As freshman, St. Ambrose went 9-0 on the way to city and state championships. As sophomores, the Cavaliers came within a minute of another perfect season, but fell to Notre Dame 27-21 in the Soup Bowl on that late punt return by Dave Baldyga. As juniors, St. Ambrose again went 9-0 on the way to city and state titles.

The Cavaliers would be breaking in a new quarterback in 1967 in Tom Cudlike, but the running of Bialk and Bob Walker would soften the departure of Greg Hacias, who headed off to the University of Nebraska on a football scholarship.

As expected, the Cavaliers romped over Bishop Gallagher, 32-6, in the opener. The second game of the season figured to be a much greater challenge — Servite, with pass-happy quarterback Frank Kolch now a junior.

Carruthers would address the opponent's strengths and weaknesses in the locker room on Mondays. He'd write the names of the opposing starters on a large classroom chalkboard and review them one by one. Only one name mattered on that chalkboard Servite week — Frank Kolch, who lit the Cavaliers up for 344 yards passing the previous season. Carruthers circled it several times for emphasis.

"He runs their offense," Carruthers said. "If we stop him, we stop Servite."

Carruthers then talked about the supporting cast. He talked about wide receiver Glen Hayner, Paul's brother, and mentioned running back Bobby Cieslak.

"Good kid," Carruthers said. "Wish we had him over here. He'd fit in."

But the Cavaliers figured to continue their quest for back-to-back city championships with a game plan geared to stopping Kolch.

"I remember carving 'Stop Kolch' into a desk at school that week," Carter said.

St. Ambrose slowed Kolch on that blazing Sunday afternoon in September. He completed only 14 of 29 passes for 185 yards. But Cieslak ripped the St. Ambrose defense to shreds with 165 yards rushing, powering Servite to 35-27 victory — its first triumph over the Cavaliers since 1955.

"We didn't have an answer for Cieslak," Carter said. "We weren't ready for him. He was unbelievable. He had all the moves. He could juke you out of your jock. We couldn't tackle him."

Ironically, Carter would room with Cieslak when the two went off to college at Wyoming.

The St. Ambrose offense was out of sync as well that day. Bialk ran a kickoff back for a touchdown for the first time in his career — but was caught from behind later in the game on another long jaunt by, who else, Cieslak. Walker lost a pass in the sun in the end zone, costing the Cavaliers another potential touchdown.

"We were stunned," said Gerry Van Goethem, the third Van Goethem of the family to play at St. Ambrose. "We didn't think we could ever lose. But it was too late for a wakeup call, as it turns out."

The next week Servite was crushed by Divine Child, 32-13. The Catholic Double-A was suddenly in the control of the Falcons, the only team still unbeaten. But a week later, the Double-A was in chaos.

St. Ambrose traveled to Dearborn on the opening weekend of October for a Sunday showdown. A former Second Division

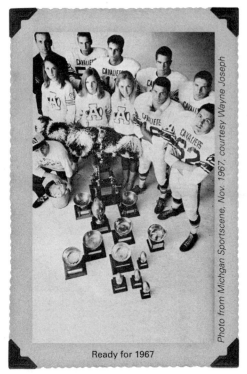

Ready for 1967

Photo from *Michgan Sportscene, Nov. 1967, courtesy Wayne Joseph*

Back row, l to r: Joe Carruthers, Nibby Skorupski, Bob Walker, Gerry (GiGi) Van Goethem, Mickey Carter; front row, l to r: St. Ambrose cheerleaders, Tom Bialk, Jonathan Reynaert; water boy Wayne Joseph

power, the Falcons were in their fifth season in the First Division but this was the first time they controlled their own destiny — win out and claim a trip to their first Soup Bowl.

It was an eerie feeling for the Cavaliers, who had lost one regular season game in four years but found themselves cast in the rare role of underdog. The entire afternoon was eerie.

"Someone was burning leaves in the neighborhood," Carter recalled. "There was smoke all over. You could hardly breathe."

But it was Divine Child that would gasp for air. Quarterback Bill Bashara committed two costly turnovers that would sink the Falcons. Carter hit Bashara as he was attempting to pass and the ball fluttered into the air, where it was intercepted by Van Goethem. The 230-pound defensive tackle lumbered 40 yards with it for a touchdown. Bob Walker also pilfered a pitchout by Bashara and returned it for score.

Walker added a 48-yard touchdown reception from Cudlike, and Bialk launched a late 75-yard quick kick that was downed inside the Divine Child 10 to squelch any comeback hopes by the Falcons.

Hayner covered a sophomore wide receiver that day by the name of Gary Danielson. The next week Divine Child coach Tony Versaci would move him to quarterback, where Danielson would lead the Falcons to three consecutive victories to close out the regular season. He would go on to play quarterback at Purdue and for 11 NFL seasons with Detroit and Cleveland.

"I guess Danielson can thank us for getting the chance to play quarterback," Carter said.

St. Ambrose didn't lose another game that season. Neither did Servite. The three teams finished in a three-way tie for the Double-A championship, but Divine Child was awarded the Soup Bowl berth based the Catholic League's tie-breaker system. So the Falcons played on to defeat Brother Rice in the Soup Bowl and Denby in the final Goodfellow Game ever played.

Divine Child won a city championship that the Cavaliers believed should have been theirs. The Ambrosians were entitled to a patch for their letter sweaters as the Catholic League Double-A tri-champion, but the players declined it. At St. Ambrose, it was all or nothing.

"We were upset," Bialk said. "We were greedy. We'd been to the playoffs three straight years and thought we were entitled to it. But when we lost to Servite, we knew that was going to be a problem. I was really disappointed we didn't get the chance to play again. That was the end of the story."

Literally.

CARRUTHERS

Joe Carruthers finished up his third season as head coach at St. Ambrose with a 22-2 record. He was winning games at a faster clip than either of his two celebrated predecessors, Tom Boisture or George Perles.

But Carruthers sensed trouble looming for little St. Ambrose. He was losing a great senior class. Center Gerry Van Goethem had been selected the school's fifth All-America. Running back Bob Walker was headed off to Michigan State and defensive lineman Mickey Carter to Wyoming.

All-state selections Tom Bialk and Sam Michaels were departing, as were Tom Cudlike, Jonathan Reynaert, and Nibby Skorupski. That group of players played an abundance of football over the previous four years for St. Ambrose and won an abundance of games.

So on the field, the Cavaliers faced a rare rebuilding season. But that wasn't a concern for Carruthers. No, his concerns were off the field. There was a cultural change taking place at St. Ambrose and in the Catholic Church that was not favoring his football team. The priests, nuns, and students were all part of that change.

Fr. Van Antwerp was the driving force in the emergence of St. Ambrose as a football power in the 1950s. But he passed away on Oct. 18, 1964 at the age of 77. The football program lost its guardian angel that day. The team knew it and paid its patriarch the ultimate tribute.

"The only day we ever took off was when Father Van Antwerp passed away and we all went to the funeral," Carruthers said.

"That's the only day I can ever recall we didn't practice."

The new priests assigned to the parish in the 1960s did not share the same passion for football as the Van Antwerps, Rozmans, Pettits and Weisners. Neither did the nuns. Perles saw it coming in 1963 when a new principal cracked down on his recruiting. The football coach no longer had carte blanche to fill up the classrooms with his football prospects.

The Catholic Church's Vatican Council II from 1962-65 contributed to the changing attitudes of the clergy.

"There was a prevailing theory in the 1960s that parochial education was an outmoded idea, that the wave of the future was to train Catholics and Christians in a more secular way rather than in a more enclosed environment like a parochial school," said Fr. Timothy Pelc, who served as the St. Ambrose pastor into the next century. "Many religious leaders bought into that in the 1960s. So you ended up with a whole wave of parishes being founded without schools. Religious education was supposed to take a more secular approach of bringing kids into the faith.

"We really walked away from arguably one of the most productive school systems the world has ever seen. Not the least of which was the faculty who walked away from that, too — the religious men and women who staffed those schools. It was no longer glamorous to be just a teacher in high school. These people wanted other jobs, other missions in the world. They wanted to expand their roles. They wanted to get involved in issues of social justice and other areas of church formation and leadership. Teaching school didn't seem to be enough any more. My guess is that a lot of the energy that was low focus in the religious orders became multiple focus."

That forced the parish schools to compete financially for lay teachers, but the money just wasn't there. Enrollment was declining, and the bottom was falling out at schools in and around

Photo courtesy Joe D'Angelo

Joe Carruthers

the Detroit city limits. The riots in 1967 triggered an urban flight that would empty out some parishes. The money wasn't there in the collection baskets to keep the churches afloat, much less the schools. The archdiocese shut down St. Catherine in 1966 and St. Anthony in 1968.

St. Ambrose was a Class C school sprinting toward Class D. Its graduating class in 1968 numbered only 68 students, the smallest of the decade.

The Cavaliers all shaved their heads as a sign of unity before the 1967 season. But hair was important to the next class — too important. The length of the sideburns, the length the hair. The age of Aquarius had arrived at St. Ambrose.

"In my last year there, all discipline seemed to be breaking down," Carruthers said. "The flower children were coming in and changing the whole neighborhood."

Fortunately for Carruthers, he had an option. A second Grosse Pointe high school was opening in 1968 to accommodate a generation of suburban baby boomers. Grosse Pointe North would be located on Eight Mile, just up the road from Lake Shore Drive.

So Carruthers phone Ed Wernet, the athletic director at North, and inquired about coaching the football team. Wernet jumped at the chance to hire a coach with Carruthers' credentials. Like Perles, Carruthers would be a three-years-and-out head coach at St. Ambrose.

"I could see what was happening at St. Ambrose," Carruthers said. "There was an increasing lack of discipline. I was going to have to fight that and not get paid for it. I could go over to Grosse Pointe and at least get paid for it."

Carruthers was earning $6,500 from St. Ambrose. North jumped his salary to $10,000. Still….

"It was tough to leave," Carruthers said. "I knew I'd never find those type of kids again. Those kids would run through walls all day long for you."

Carruthers would take over a football program with no history, no tradition, no returning starters, and no senior class. Carruthers was recruiting a grade-school quarterback named Joe Puleo for St. Ambrose but took him to North when he switched allegiances. Puleo would go on to earn a scholarship to Northwestern.

Joe D'Angelo replaced Carruthers as the head coach at St. Ambrose, and the two arranged for a scrimmage that fall between the two schools.

"We had the best facilities in the country at the time," said Carruthers of Grosse Pointe North. "I wanted to show my kids the facilities St. Ambrose had. We drove by the school and the windows were all open and the kids were yelling out. I asked Joe, 'What's going on?' And he said, 'That's the new thinking by the new principal.' I thought, 'You're in trouble, Joe.'"

And he was.

D'ANGELO

George Perles played football at Michigan State. His goal in life was to return there one day as a coach. That was Joe D'Angelo's dream on a lesser scale — he was a football hero at St. Ambrose and wanted to one day return to Hampton Road as a coach.

Joe Carruthers gave D'Angelo that opportunity in 1965, hiring him as an assistant even though he had not yet graduated from the University of Detroit. D'Angelo still needed to fulfill his student-teaching requirement at Hillger Elementary School in Detroit. But with degree in hand in 1966, his duties expanded at St. Ambrose to coach/teacher. Then D'Angelo became Carruthers' top assistant in 1967 when Jeff Hartman left to coach in Midland.

When Carruthers bolted to become the head coach at Grosse Pointe North in 1968, D'Angelo found himself in his dream job — the head coach of perennial Catholic League power St. Ambrose. His fourth-down touchdown in the 1959 Goodfellow Game put the Cavaliers on the city's football map, and now D'Angelo was charged with keeping them there.

When Perles took over from Tom Boisture in 1962, he immediately put his stamp on St. Ambrose. Out went the finesse offense of Boisture. Power football was now in. When Carruthers took over for Perles in 1965, he immediately put his stamp on the team. Out went that steady diet of student body right and student body left of the Perles era. Aerial football was now in.

But when D'Angelo took over from Carruthers, the young coach decided his best chance for success was to maintain the status quo. Keep the same offense, the same defense and just out-work and out-execute everyone like the Cavaliers had been doing throughout the 1960s.

"That was a way of life," D'Angelo said. "That was our system. I tried to follow the same formula that got St. Ambrose where it was."

That was a mistake. D'Angelo didn't have the same caliber of players the Cavaliers had been fielding the entire decade. After 19-12 season-opening victory over Benedictine, St. Ambrose lost five consecutive games on the way to a 2-5 record. The Cavaliers had never lost five games in a season, much less five in a row.

"We didn't have great talent that year," Paul Hayner said. "We had some toughness but not a lot of skill. That [season] was an embarrassment because of the great tradition there."

The gap was widening between St. Ambrose, Servite, and Divine Child. Gary Danielson was now a full-blown star at Divine Child and the Falcons smoked the Cavaliers, 34-19. Frank Kolch was already a star and continued to torment St. Ambrose with his arm, passing Servite to a 26-6 victory.

"Frank was the greatest high-school athlete I've ever seen," Hayner said. "No way were we going to beat Servite or Divine Child. They were the class of the league."

In 1967, the St. Ambrose Dad's Club resurrected the school's hockey team after five years of dormancy. The parish kids were falling through the cracks during the St. Ambrose recruiting frenzy of the 1960s. Perles and Carruthers were bringing in the best football players from other parishes to represent the school. The hockey team would give talented parish kids such as Pete Sudnick, Tim Griffin, Ken Fagan, and Dan Setter the chance to wear the school colors and earn varsity letters.

The Dad's Club bought the uniforms for the hockey team but that was the extent of its financial commitment. The players themselves had to purchase their own equipment and pay for ice time.

St. Ambrose was the only hockey team in the city to call Canada home. The Cavaliers rented out Windsor Arena across the Detroit River for its home games and once-weekly practice sessions. D'Angelo served as the coach.

St. Ambrose didn't win a game in its first year but inside of three seasons was competing with the best teams in the city. In the 1968 state tournament, the Cavaliers lost to St. Clair Shores Lakeview, the No. 1 team in the state, 2-0 on two goals in the game's final five minutes. St. Ambrose would upset traditional powers Cranbrook, Lake Shore, and South Lake and in 1969 captured a Second Division championship. It would be the last title won by any St. Ambrose team in any sport. The school's hockey team won more games (7) that school year than the rest of the boys' varsity sports combined. St. Ambrose dropped the program following that season.

Frank Crachiolo become the last St. Ambrose athlete drafted by any professional team in 1969, ironically, in baseball — the worst sport at the school. He had been captain of the school's football and basketball teams but the Detroit Tigers drafted him in the 22nd round in 1969 as a catcher.

The archdiocese closed another handful of schools in 1969, including Cathedral, Salesian, St. Martin, and St. Philip. The latter two were neighboring parishes of St. Ambrose on the Detroit side of Alter Road.

St. Ambrose was in a football hole, and the Catholic League dug it a little deeper. A change in the scheduling format called for teams in the Double-A to open the season with two games against teams from the Central Division. Those were all-boys schools and all were triple the enrollment of St. Ambrose.

The Cavaliers drew defending Central Division champion University of Detroit and emerging Brother Rice for their two crossover games. D'Angelo knew status quo wouldn't work in 1969, so he finally put his stamp on the Cavaliers. Quietly, behind

Photo courtesy Tom Boisture, from Detroit News

Joe D'Angelo

the closed doors of the hall, D'Angelo implemented the Houston veer offense.

The quarterback would take the snap and it was his option where the ball would go based on his read of the defensive end. If the end cracked down, the quarterback would fake to the full-back and continue down the line, either turning upfield himself or pitching the ball to a trailing halfback. If the defensive end stood up and held his ground on the edge of the line, the quarterback would hand the ball to the fullback inside.

"I thought I had the perfect fullback for that offense in Paul Hayner," D'Angelo said.

Hayner started at cornerback on defense and played all the skill positions except quarterback in his first three varsity seasons.

D'Angelo planned to strap the offense to his back in 1969. Hayner would line up at fullback on running downs and move to wide receiver in passing situations.

The Cavaliers traveled to the University of Detroit for the opener. The Cubs were not prepared for the new offense, and St. Ambrose literally ran away with a 28-14 victory.

"It was unbelievable," Hayner said. "There were such huge holes. I wouldn't be touched for 20 yards. They were always biting on the pitch."

But the next week against Brother Rice, quarterback Mark Sopoliga left the game with an injury, and the Cavaliers couldn't generate any offense in an 18-8 loss. Victories over Redford St. Mary and Shrine set up a Double-A showdown in Dearborn against Divine Child. Both teams took 3-1 records into the game — but that didn't mean the two were evenly matched. The Falcons returned the game's opening kickoff for a touchdown and never stopped scoring, winning 32-0.

"They had better players and better coaches than we did," Hayner said.

Indeed. Michigan State hired Divine Child head coach Tony Versaci in 1970, so the Falcons promoted their defensive coordinator. Bill McCartney went on to coach Divine Child to both a state basketball and football championship in 1973 and Colorado to an NCAA football championship in 1990. He also founded the Promise Keepers in 1990.

St. Ambrose won out in 1969, finishing 6-2.

"It wasn't a vintage Ambrose team," Hayner said, "but we were good."

Hayner turned down a scholarship from Nebraska to play offense in favor of an offer from Michigan State to play defense. Ironically, Versaci would be his freshman coach in 1970.

Hayner earned all-city and all-state honors in both football and basketball at St. Ambrose. His letter sweater bore 12 stripes — four whites for lettering, five yellows for all-city and three reds for all-state.

When Hayner graduated, the last great athlete of the St. Ambrose football legacy left the building. He started for three years at Michigan State, leading the Big Ten in interceptions in 1972. He reached the final cut in training camp with the Buffalo Bills in 1974 in his quest to become the third Cavalier to play in the NFL.

The Catholic school closings continued. The archdiocese decreed that if a school couldn't sustain itself financially, it could not keep its doors open. Among those shutting down in 1970 were St. Stanislaus and St. Paul, St. Ambrose's neighbor to the East.

The money and aura were drying up simultaneously on the Cavaliers. A 1-7 season in 1970 signaled the end. The archdiocese announced St. Ambrose would close its doors after the 1971-72 school year. D'Angelo tried to fight it. He was not ready to concede his Camelot.

"My wife and I were emotionally attached to that school," D'Angelo said. "So we took it upon ourselves to raise money. I remember staging the boxing matches — and this time selling tickets to the public. Anything we could do to raise money to keep the school open, we were willing to try."

D'Angelo recalls attending a parish meeting in the church. The evening was a disaster. He witnessed a meltdown by a parish.

"I was appalled that people were so disrespectful — we were in the church, mind you — screaming at the priests because the school was going to close down," D'Angelo said.

Action, D'Angelo believed, could keep the school open. Not words. So he was prepared to wage that fight. If it meant more paper drives, more 50-50 raffles, more boxing matches to generate the money to keep the school afloat, so be it. But this was not a fight D'Angelo could win with the archdiocese.

Demolishing St. Ambrose

Photo courtesy Dave Vitali, by Grosse Pointe News

"I was the bridge between the old St. Ambrose and present day," D'Angelo said. "I think they came to resent me. They literally cut my position out. They didn't fire me, but they got rid of me by eliminating phys ed from the curriculum. I was the phys ed teacher and athletic director — and they cut out the position. So I didn't have a job. They wanted to get rid of the person who was stoking the fire about keeping the school open.

"It was disheartening. You could see it coming. I found out you can't fight city hall."

St. Ambrose hired Harvey Heitman to serve as head coach for its farewell football season in 1971. The Cavaliers would compete as a Class D school with fewer than 300 students. St. Ambrose went winless and scoreless, losing to East Catholic 6-0, Austin 12-

0, DeLaSalle 7-0, Servite 20-0, Bishop Gallagher 16-0, Redford St. Mary 36-0, Shrine 25-0, and Divine Child 36-0.

"We had no bodies," Heitman said. "I think we had only 25-26 kids with no freshman or sophomore class to speak of... I called the Catholic League before the season and asked if they would let us drop down a division so we could compete. They said no. I felt everyone wanted to get their whacks in at St. Ambrose and this was their chance."

Hayner recalled walking onto the practice field at Michigan State in October 1971. Defensive line coach Ed Youngs approached him, smile on his face.

"Hey, Paul," Youngs cackled. "Who's going to be the MVP at St. Ambrose this year — the first runner to cross the 50-yard line?"

That stung Hayner.

"There was so much pride about Ambrose and all the colleges knew it," Hayner said. "For it to go down like that...it was sad, really sad."

Twelve years later, in October 1983, a wrecking ball did what so many parochial and public school football rivals in the 1950s and '60s could not — pummel St. Ambrose. By the end of the day, the building was a pile of rubble. The school was gone.

But not the memory of a truly great high-school football program.

"I told my four sons St. Ambrose was the best thing that ever happened to me," Greg Hacias said. "St. Ambrose, George Perles, and Joe Carruthers opened many, many doors for me — and they are still being opened today.

"As a retired executive of General Motors, when I introduce myself, people say, 'Hacias...Hacias...Hacias... did you play at St. Ambrose?' Forty years later, people still remember St. Ambrose. It's amazing how many executives — guys making half a million dollars — want to talk St. Ambrose football."

St. Ambrose may be gone. But not the legacy.

EPILOGUE

When Joe D'Angelo was the head football coach at Detroit Country Day in the 1990s, he pushed for admission into the Detroit Catholic League.

Country Day established itself as a formidable football presence in Detroit, winning a state title in both the 1980s and 1990s under D'Angelo. To stay on top, D'Angelo knew through his own personal experience at St. Ambrose that you needed to continue playing the biggest and best teams.

Country Day had played the occasional Catholic League team throughout D'Angelo's tenure as coach (Bishop Gallagher, Notre Dame, and the University of Detroit) plus some of the best Catholic teams from around the state (Jackson Lumen Christi, Muskegon Catholic Central, and Monroe St. Mary).

But D'Angelo believed Country Day could maximize its potential by playing Detroit Catholic League teams on an annual basis. Even though Country Day was a private school, D'Angelo wanted to compete with the Catholics.

So D'Angelo led a Country Day contingent to the Catholic League offices in downtown Detroit to plead his case.

"We're in this big room," D'Angelo recalled, "and I knew a lot of the people in that room. They told us, 'We don't want you guys in our league because you recruit.'"

D'Angelo had to stifle a laugh.

"I called them a bunch of hypocrites," he said. "I said, 'You guys all recruited. I was part of the Catholic League when we recruited, so don't give me that. I know you did then and you still do now." That shut them up. They said they would allow us in under one condition — we couldn't compete for the Catholic League championship.

"We're still not in, but we're playing basically a Catholic League schedule with the U. of D., Catholic Central, Brother Rice, Orchard Lake St. Mary...the best there is."

You might say St. Ambrose wrote the Catholic League book on recruiting. Starting with Tom Boisture's first class featuring D'Angelo and Manny Lamprides, the Cavaliers leaned heavily on their mercenaries for gridiron success.

"Most of the guys who started were hand-picked and weren't even from the parish," Paul Hayner said. "We had guys from CYO programs all over the city."

St. Ambrose also wrote the book on winning. The Cavaliers were the most successful team of the Goodfellow era with a 5-0 record in those city championship games. The only other schools that did not lose a Goodfellow Game in the event's 30-year history were Redford (2-0), DeLaSalle (1-0), Divine Child (1-0), and MacKenzie (1-0). Denby went to a record nine Goodfellow Games but won only four of them. Redford St. Mary set a Catholic League record with eight appearances but also won just three times.

The public-school champion was shut out in only five of the 30 Goodfellow Games. St. Ambrose authored three of the shutouts. The Cavaliers also played in front of the largest crowd in Goodfellow history and three of the top five crowds. There was magic in the St. Ambrose name and the St. Ambrose way.

When Joe Carruthers left St. Ambrose for Grosse Pointe North in 1968, his initial priority was to establish a Dad's Club. His first call went out to an old friend — fellow Michigan State alumnus Bob "Buck" McCurry, the general manager at Dodge.

"He lived in the Grosse Pointe district and his kids were going to attend the new high school, so I went down to see him," Carruthers said. "I talked to him about raising funds so we could do some of the things we did at St. Ambrose — the pre-game dinners, the letter jackets and things like that.

"He gave me a brand new Dodge so I raffled it off. I had some of the fathers help me with it and damn if we didn't raise $15,000. We started the same thing we had at St. Ambrose over at Grosse Pointe North. It was taking a little of that Ambrose tradition over to Grosse Pointe."

It was the same with D'Angelo. He may have left St. Ambrose in 1971 — but St. Ambrose never left him. He incorporated the St. Ambrose way at his next coaching stop at Erie Mason.

"We did things to emulate the Catholic League even though it was a public school," D'Angelo said. "On Fridays we'd have a pep rally. After that we walked over to church. It wasn't that far. Even though a lot of them weren't Catholic and I told them they didn't have to go, almost all of them went. We'd have the priest give us a blessing.

"My wife would take over the school kitchen and make a spaghetti sauce, and we'd go back over there and have our pre-game meal. I started a Dad's Club, just like at St. Ambrose. I took that whole St. Ambrose philosophy and transferred it down there. I carried the same thing with me to Country Day — the team meals, the prayer. In a lot of ways, it still felt like I was at St. Ambrose."

D'Angelo would go on to become one of the most successful football coaches in state history, gaining enshrinement in the Michigan High School Football Coaches Association (MHSFCA) Hall of Fame with his 205 career victories. Only nine came at St. Ambrose; the rest came at Erie Mason and Country Day. D'Angelo coached Country Day to state Class C championships in 1986 and 1995. Erie Mason also would go on to win a state title in the 1980s.

Al Fracassa left Shrine in 1969 to become the head coach at Birmingham Brother Rice, where he would win six state championships — three in the 1980s, one in the 1990s and two in the

2000s. He's also enshrined in the MHSFCA Hall of Fame, as is Harvey Heitman. He overcame that 0-8 start to his coaching career at St. Ambrose to win more than 100 games, primarily at Redford Union.

Divine Child would replace St. Ambrose as the dominant co-ed school in the Catholic League, winning state titles on the field in 1975 and 1985. The Falcons won their championships by surviving state playoffs. The four state titles won by St. Ambrose were mythical. Hayner believes the Cavaliers would have claimed even more championships in the 1960s had they been required to win them on the field.

"We were always playing schools bigger than us," Hayner said. "We were always the smallest enrollment school on the field. If they had state playoffs back then, that would have been great. Instead of beating all Class A and Class B schools, we'd have to beat schools our size for championships. I'd like our chances."

Tom Boisture, George Perles, John Thursby, and Heitman all gained admission to the Catholic League Hall of Fame. So did St. Ambrose assistants Miles Currie and Jim Plecas, plus rivals Fracassa, Walt Bazylewicz, Frank Buford, Jack Carroll, Mike D'Angelo, Nick Galante, Ed Lauer, Bill McCartney, and Tony Versaci. Former St. Ambrose players Joe Spada and Ron Biotti also were enshrined as coaches.

In 1980, the Catholic League inducted John Tobianski into its Hall of Fame posthumously for distinguished service. To this day he remains the only janitor enshrined. Tobianski died in September 1969 of heart failure, at the age of 55. Perles, Carruthers, and a generation of St. Ambrose players paid their respects at his funeral.

"The pallbearers were all football players," Kathy Tobianski said. "There were rows and rows of guys wearing their letter sweaters. The church was packed — and there was a lot of maroon in the pews."

That same church, where so many Cavaliers attended so many Masses and said so many prayers in the 1950s and '60s, was later featured in the Clint Eastwood movie "Gran Torino," released in 2008.

Boisture's keen eye for talent evaluation developed as a CYO basketball referee in the 1950s served him well in the 1980s when he became the personnel director of the New York Giants. His draft boards produced the likes of Lawrence Taylor, Joe Morris, Leonard Marshall, Carl Banks, Mark Bavaro, Pepper Johnson, and Rodney Hampton, who provided the backbone of teams that would win NFL championships in the 1986 and 1990 seasons.

Boisture hired Jerry Reese in 1994 as a scout for the Giants. Reese would go on to replace Boisture as director of personnel in 2002 on his way to general manager in 2007. Working under Boisture, Reese discovered the tough love Boisture once showed his high-school football players.

"I thought Tom was hard on me with my evaluations," Reese said. "I thought he critiqued me hard. But I realized he was trying to make me better. He critiqued all of us hard. He made us all better scouts."

Perles' smash-mouth coaching style served him well in the 1970s when he became the defensive-line coach of the Pittsburgh Steelers. He molded Joe Greene, L.C. Greenwood, Dwight White, and Ernie Holmes into a Steel Curtain that provided the impetus for four Super Bowls that decade.

"George used to talk about St. Ambrose all the time," said Greene, a Pro Football Hall of Famer. "He used to say after he left St. Ambrose, everything else in his life was gravy."

In 2000, the Detroit Free Press selected an all-time high-school football team for its Detroit Almanac. Tom Beer, Dan Currie, and Joe Henze were named to the team along with one of the Pacioreks, Jim of Orchard Lake St. Mary.

St. Joan of Arc was very good to St. Ambrose, sending D'Angelo, Bill Fournier, Dave Kulinski, Ray Malcoun, Cory Richardson, Steve Himberg, and Gary Nowak down to Hampton Road to start on city championship teams. St. Ambrose returned the favor in the 1970s. Spada coached the St. Joan eighth-graders to their first perfect season (7-0) in 1970 and Dave Vitali guided the Chargers to their second perfect season (8-0) in 1973.

St. Ambrose also gave back to Grosse Pointe. Greg Hacias served a stint in the 1990s as president of the Grosse Pointe Park Little League. His empire was the four baseball diamonds at Defer, where he once spent his falls practicing football as the St. Ambrose quarterback.

St. Ambrose provided a bonding experience for families. Malcoun's older brother Tony was stricken with polio, and his father did not want Ray to play football as a grade schooler.

"His belief was you went to school to study, not to play sports," Ray said.

But his mother and brother pleaded Ray's case to his father, who relented and let him try out for the St. Joan of Arc team in the sixth grade.

"Now fast forward that to the Ambrose days," Malcoun said. "I started as a sophomore and I could see my dad on the sideline, walking up and down. He had a little grocery store two blocks from Mack Park on Lillibridge and Canfield — Joe's Market. He had it open 12 hours a day. But on Saturday nights he'd put a sign in the window, 'Closed — see you at the game.'

"The fact it was so close to my dad's store made it even more special for me. The customers would come in Sunday mornings and say, 'I see where your boy's team won again.' That's my fondest memory. This was a dad who did not want me to play football."

St. Ambrose provided countless opportunities for children of blue-collar families to forge white-collar lives. Mickey Carter earned All-Catholic honors as a senior and parlayed his football talent into a scholarship to Wyoming. He served as a team captain there as a senior, graduated with a degree in education and returned to Michigan where he would spend more than three decades as a teacher in the Detroit Public School system.

"Going to St. Ambrose was a life-changing experience," Carter said. "No one in my family ever went to college. My two older brothers went to work for Dodge Main.

"But when I was a junior and saw some of the seniors going off to college, I thought, 'You know, I think I'm as good as that guy.' That's when I started thinking about college. I'd have never gone to college had it not been for St. Ambrose. My life would have been totally different than what it is now. I would have not been the same person."

St. Ambrose straightened out lives. Tom Bialk attended different schools in the seventh and eighth grades. He was one of only two freshmen to letter on the 1964 Goodfellow champions, and Carruthers later confided that he and Perles felt compelled to play the talented Bialk because they weren't sure he would even be around for his sophomore season.

"I was a hellion," Bialk conceded. "I was headed down the wrong road with the wrong group of people. I was on the edge. There were kids I grew up with who died of heroin overdoses and went to jail for murder. My mother told me you're going to a Catholic school because you need discipline.

"St. Ambrose gave me the opportunity to get a good education, play sports, meet people and understand a different lifestyle because the school was in Grosse Pointe. Having those types of friends opened up a whole new world to me. All of a sudden Tony Piccione and I were running around together taking the bus back and forth to school. Greg Hacias was stopping by to pick me up for school. It moved me into a different realm of people, some great men. It made a complete difference in my life. It gave me an opportunity I never would have had."

Bialk graduated from Wayne State in special education. He would use his degree to serve as a special education director, vocational director, assistant principal, and finally a principal at schools. He also coached some football, twice taking teams to the state playoffs.

"Both times we got beat by Catholic schools — surprise, surprise," Bialk said.

St. Ambrose created a level of expectation for the Cavaliers — and those who competed against them. Mike Ward retired up north to Houghton Lake later in life and was active in the Elks. As an officer, he was the point person one year for the lodge's entry in the ritual contest at the state convention.

"I'm nervous as can be," Ward said, "and a fellow comes up to me and says, 'Is your name Mike Ward?' I said yeah, and he said, 'You went to St. Ambrose, didn't you?' I said yeah again, and he said, 'Then you're going to win this thing.'

"And I did."

St. Ambrose taught its players compassion. When Marshall Houle's father Bernard died in the summer of 1960, Boisture trooped the entire football team to Verheyden Funeral Home for visitation and the rosary. Mike Goff came from a family of nine kids. When his father suffered a construction accident that prevented him from working one summer, Boisture put Goff to work as Tobianski's assistant.

"I'd polish the shoes, refurbish the equipment, go to the dry cleaners, wash the bus, wash Boisture's car — whatever John wanted me to do," Goff said. "I got paid $1 an hour. The check was written on the athletic association's bank account and signed by Fr. Weisner. It was cash, no taxes, $40 a week. With my father out of work, that helped us out a lot."

In 2003, after Boisture retired from the New York Giants, the Cavaliers staged a football reunion at the Knights of Columbus Hall in Detroit. It was a who's who of St. Ambrose gridiron greatness: Boisture, Perles, D'Angelo, Ron Albers, both Greg and Larry Bringard, Jim Conahan, Jack Cairo, Ray Federspiel, Bill Fournier, Mike Goff, Marshall Houle, Larry Lantzy, Skip Paoletti, both Mike and Vince Taormino, Mike Van Goethem, Dave Vitali....

In subsequent reunions Tom Beer returned along with fellow All-Americas Bill Lenhard and Gerry Van Goethem. Joe Carruthers, Lloyd Bayer, Dave Brozo, Norm Cure, Jim Dinverno, John Jambor, Jim Laskowski, Pete Piazza, Sam Serra, and Gerry Stogniew all came back. Forty and 50 years after celebrating championships, the coaches and players of St. Ambrose gathered to reminisce about some magical moments in time.

"St. Ambrose was a special place," Bialk said. "I felt privileged to go there."

And wear the maroon and white.

"I've played major college football and in the NFL," Beer said. "I've played in a lot of big games. But those Goodfellow Games are my fondest experiences as a football player. Every bit of sweat and blood we dropped in the summertime was worth it that night. You'll never forget those nights for as long as you live."